Light and Glory: Shine

God's Valiant Warrior

Light and Glory: Shine

God's Valiant Warrior

Shining out of the darkness of deception and godlessness of abuse to reveal His glory and kingdom.

A Time to Shine

KAREN L. JOHNSON

Copyright Information

Light and Glory: Shine-God's Valiant Warrior
By: Karen L. Johnson

ISBN-13: 978-1-888081-38-1
ISBN-10: 1-888081-38-4

Unless otherwise indicated, all Scripture quotations are from the Authorized King James Version of the Bible.

Printed in the United States of America

Victorious Life Foundation, International
PO Box 1628
Elk City, OK 73648
580.821.2410
Graceplace2009@gmail.com
www.thevictoriouslife.org

Format and Cover Design by Lisa Buck
lisa.joy.buck@gmail.com

DISCLAIMER

Disclaimer to the contents in this Book.

The information and memories expressed in this book cover 25 years of deliverance, inner healing sessions, prayer sessions, biblical counseling, years of bible studies and devotionals, anointed services with preaching and a choice to be faithful to God's word and His will for my wholeness.

Generational curses are very real and along with the cult iniquities of my European heritage have proven to be formidable challenges to walking free.

Yet, my Moravian prayer heritage allowed for an intercessory prayer call on my life and my Jewishness heritage a call to pray for the peace of Jerusalem, Israel and Palestine.

Some of us are more drawn to the dark side than others depending on the type of spiritual covenants our parents agreed to and followed. Vows to secret societies are dangerous and open doors to the powers of darkness whether knowingly or unknowingly to the 4 th generation.

Societies and doctrines supporting racism and anti-Semitic beliefs cause generations of hatred buried deep in the mind and hearts of the people.

When abuse takes place one always asks the obvious question, "Who knew about this?"

The answer is buried in our sin nature. Most people know abuse happens.

Fear and shame are great silencers but pride, power and the predator always win the trophies.

—Karen Johnson

TRIBUTE

This work of love is a tribute to the men and women who have fought for freedom for our country so we may live free in Christ Jesus.

My father, George R. Holdorf, Sr., Sergeant, 95th Infantry Div, Co. L, one of the Iron Men of Metz, France, and holder of the Soldiers Medal of valor and courage in the line of duty.

My husband, Tom M. Johnson, LTC, Airborne Ranger, US Army Retired, Bronze Star Medal for Vietnam.

My brother, George R. Holdorf, Jr., Sergeant, US Tank Command, Desert Storm.

DEDICATION

I am forever thankful for the many intercessors and ministers whom God has put in my life to pray for my freedom and to persevere in service to Christ no matter what the cost. I believe in divine appointments and connections that God ordained to bring me through the battles of abuse to transformation. The words of personal prophecies and God's Word prevailed to encourage me to have faith to see the mountains move, my mind transformed, deep healing in my heart and the false belief system in my mind torn down. For the Lord spoke that He and He alone had woven me into a tapestry of great beauty with a gold thread defining His glory and mark on my life that He had done the weaving and was the Master of the design

FOREWORD

After being on God's path of mercy and grace for years, it is important to acknowledge what only He can do if we are willing to take on the challenge to change by following Christ. As a servant of God, it was significant to press through to breakthrough in every area of my life that was not submitted to God's will. This was a formidable challenge and journey.

God's word, God's love, and God's grace brought me through the valley of the shadow of death to His great light of salvation. I am eternally grateful for God's intervention, to see His plan and His path for my life brought into alignment with Heaven. Not only did I experience revelations about Christ, but His everlasting covenant of grace. Grace is the heartbeat of the Father using us to love others to faith.

May you be touched by the testimony. My prayer for you is that the Holy Spirit will breathe life into you as He did me along the path of following God's will. Let your life goal be to love as many as you can into His Kingdom. Embrace the single obsession to seek the hungry and the lost.

– Karen L. Johnson

CONTENTS

INTRODUCTION TO HIS DIVINE EXCHANGE

Within these pages lies my testimony of God's incredible love, mercy, and grace toward a sinner saved miraculously. With no one else to deliver me from death's grip I cried out to Him, "Help me, God!" And oh, He did.

December 26, 1986 my midnight cry was heard by my heavenly Father. Satan wanted my life and I could feel the weight of his concrete grave over me to be my destiny. A Ferris wheel of suicidal thoughts came reeling in my mind to kill myself, do it just do it. When I turned to my husband he said "pray to your God for help" and so I made that choice. My eyes were opened to the spirit and before me was an abyss with Jesus Christ standing on one side and me on the other. He told me to "press in with great faith to HIM to reach out and grab His hand of mercy". I did. He brought me to the other side of the abyss with Him and when I came into realization I found myself sitting up in my bed singing Jesus loves me this I know for the bible tells me so. The heavenly visitation lasted 3 hours.

I am living what God spoke through the prophet Jeremiah in chapter 1, verse 5:

"Before I formed you in the womb I knew you..."

God truly does not make mistakes. He does choose to have us born and be used by Him on the earth as a witness to His faithfulness.

> *"The Lord thy God in the midst of thee is mighty; He will save, he will rejoice over thee with joy; He will rest in his love; he will joy over thee with singing." – Zephaniah 3:17*

Who would open the door to the spirit world for such a visitation and rescue from death's assignment? Answer: Jesus Christ of Nazareth knows the whole truth of one's life and destiny.

I drew a time-line of my life's significant events.

To my dismay there were areas I could not remember. Conception to 5 years of age was dark. Why? Looking at pictures of my childhood didn't help me. Investigating my family history helped but there was still a blank. There appeared to be no memory which was odd. Lord, shine your light in my darkness I prayed. He did.

My parents were both abuse survivors who married young and divorced early in their marriage due to infidelity by my father who had returned from World War 2 severely traumatized with PTSD. My mother, sister and brother and I moved in with my grandparents who were faithful to introduce me to God at an early age of 4 years old. They took me to Sunday school, church, vacation Bible school, and youth classes. I have been told in the 1950's it was required in the divorce decree to raise the children as Christians. This was all happening parallel to the ritual abuse of the occult. The goodness of God and pain of the occult became confused in my mind.

I had knowledge of the Word of God every Sunday throughout the first 15 years of my life but the deadness in me from being victimized brought rebellion and rejection. Because of the effectiveness of the trauma I had amnesia and severe fears. I had no conscious memory of what had been done to me in secret.

In high school my best friend was told she could no long associate with me because I came from a broken home-my parents were divorced. My friend came from a Catholic family and the father took a very strong stand. Catholics do not believe in divorce. I could no longer be with my best childhood friend. On a visit back to MD to see my mother, God orchestrated the forgiveness of the father to me in a Bel Air, MD shopping mall. He could not wait to ask for my forgiveness for rejecting me as a teenager because of what my parents did. All four of his children had experienced divorce. He wept.

I chose to focus on my scholastic achievement and made National Honor Society.

At 19 I left home after getting married and with child. Without having yet asked Jesus to be my Savior, and with hidden abuses still to be uncovered, my soul was filled with great darkness and an absolute deadness. There remained the huge need to be loved, accepted, and secure; I sought after God.

I continued down life's path like most of us do with family, relationships, college, and a career with the Department of Defense. I divorced after twelve years of marriage from my first husband and I remained single until I was in my mid-thirties working as a consultant/analyst. I am married to my current husband who I met in the Pentagon in 1981. He was single and had custody of his three children who were eight, ten, and twelve. We lived in Little Rock, AR for three years and moved to Elk City, OK, in 1985.

We found a lovely home and began a life together. But each of us suffered from the relocation to a small town not only saying good bye to new friends in Arkansas but the shock of a small town starting over to find friends took us for a surprise.

I knew in my "knower" that I would not survive being a stepmother without God being firmly in the center of all the relationships. I loved my husband, but I knew that I needed God's supernatural love to come into my heart so that I could love another's child.

Love was the key, but I had not experienced the agape love of God, the Father, in all my 34 years. When I did experience it a few years later at a local Aglow meeting, I melted into His loving arms. The guest speaker's intercessor came over to me in obedience to God, folded her arms around me, and said, "God wants you to know how much He loves you." And she released His liquid supernatural love that penetrated my soul. I prayed and asked God, what it takes to have that kind of compassion and intense love for another. God whispered, ask to be made an intercessor, a bond servant for My glory and so I did.

God knew I was surviving, hanging on by a thread – a mustard seed of faith – believing that what I was taught as a child about God and the gospel of Christ was real – that God was real. I had not personally experienced the Holy Spirit's power by going to church services. I was going through all the steps to believe, but when I actually experienced the unbelievable love of God, nothing – absolutely nothing take its place. There are no substitutes. Only God can fill the void. He wires our DNA in the womb for destiny in His kingdom to be loved, to be secure, and to know Him more and more and more. To be more Christ-like every day is a wonderful goal.

My daily walk with God has evolved over the years to have faith and fight the good fight of faith. It turned out Elk City is an oasis of God's compassion and love because of the high concentration of Christians per capita. God knows best in putting one right where they are supposed to be to get a breakthrough from the past.

I did not know how to recognize His voice every time. It was a learning process that He took me through with great faith, love and patience. How rewarding it is to realize along the way that you are growing in your knowledge of Him and learning more and more the depths of His love for you.

I came out of a background of much emotional pain and suffering of loss of relationships. Great sadness existed deep within. But why?

Real Christian life and wholeness seemed bigger than I was, stronger than I could ever be, impossible for me to come into freedom, healing and reality. I was surrounded by loving Christian women and families in Elk City, OK. What was blocking the fullness of love? My pain and how much pain do I have. I wanted to be rid of it and get unstuck.

It was suggested that I role play with another person to just relate. To my shock I was paralyzed with fear and could not form words or thoughts.

I began searching scriptures in the Word of God that spoke to my heart, so personally. Here are a few of them.

2 Corinthians 5:17:

> *"Therefore if any man be in Christ, he is a new creature: old things are passed away; behold all things are become new."*

1 Samuel 2:9:

> *"He will keep the feet of his saints, and the wicked shall be silent in darkness; For by strength shall no man prevail?"*

2 Thessalonians 3:3:

> *"But the Lord is faithful, who shall establish you, and keep you from evil."*

Through 2 Corinthians 7:8 I learned that sometimes it is right and proper for us to be corrected by the Word in order for us to grow properly before the Lord. I caught that in Paul's words here:

> *"For though I made you sorry with a letter, I do not repent, though I did repent: for I perceive that the same epistle hath made you sorry, though it was but for a season."*

Ephesians 1:17:

> *"...That the God of our Lord Jesus Christ, the Father of glory, may give unto you the spirit of wisdom and revelation in the knowledge of him."*

Galatians 5:20-23:

"[20] "Idolatry, witchcraft, hatred, variance, emulations, wrath, strife, seditions, heresies, [21] envying, murders, drunkenness, reveling, and such like: of the which I tell you before, as I have also told you in time past, that they which do such things shall not inherit the kingdom of God. [22] But the fruit of the Spirit is love, joy, peace, long-suffering, gentleness, goodness, faith, [23] meekness, and temperance: against such there is no law."

In 1 Corinthians 13 I learned how the love of God was designed to operate through me as a believer. In the 61st chapter of Isaiah I learned more of what took place in my spirit in that great exchange we call salvation. Jesus took all my sin and death on Himself for me and gave me abundant life in its place. And if that weren't enough, He gave me love, purpose and a reason for being. I am convinced it will take us forever to be able to fathom the depths of His love for us and all that He accomplished for us on that cross. I am eternally grateful that He did it. What an awesome Savior. What a mighty God.

In those earlier days of my adventure with God, I read also in Revelation chapter 4, in Joel chapter 2, and all through Joshua a clear call from God to choose this day that you will serve. And I knew I had to make a decision: would I choose to serve the pain of the past or would I leave it with Jesus and move on in newness of life in Him? Serve the pain or serve God. Sounds pretty cut and dry, and in one sense it is. And yet, when dealing with the fears of the flesh, it's not quite that simple.

Matthew 6:33:

"But seek ye first the kingdom of God, and his righteousness; and all these things shall be added unto you."

I head this scripture from maintenance man at a big church nearby at a time when I was so confused and not sure what direction to follow.

Well, I took his advice and began the journey of seeking the Lord with all of my heart.

The first thing God had me do was to look up the word "seek." Then He led me to watch my husband's bird dogs being trained to find quail. The Lord said just as the dog gives his whole being to seek out the quail, I was to seek Him with my whole heart, soul, and mind. I pondered this because I was so new to being a Spirit-filled Christian at the time. All I knew to do was to pray and ask God for the next step and believe that I was hearing Him.

It wasn't too long until I heard "pain drives your train." He went on to say, "Your emotional pain from the past is the driving force in you, not My Spirit." Isn't it interesting that we can be so zealous for God, but miss Him if blinded by deep pain? Deep calls to deep and so I pursued emotional healing from anything and everything as God revealed it to me. As traumatic childhood memories and flashbacks would be exposed gently. One-by-one I took them to the Lord in prayer and to counseling sessions. Slowly, day by day my life began to change like a butterfly coming out of a cocoon. Sometimes negative thoughts would bubble up in me so I would know to renew my mind with God's word.

"Park at the ark of My presence" was the next strong word I heard. This led me to enroll in Precept Bible Studies to learn the Word for myself, letting God teach me His truths. It is a glorious thing to hear the voice of God. He kept calling my name in the night hours and I would get up and sit with Him. Many times I spent with Him from four in the morning until sunrise. It was wonderful.

His Word is like a diamond – multi-faceted, shining in the light. The light produces a rainbow and the rainbow means covenant, surrounding His throne. I was led to study covenant, and as I did, I was taken back to the many truths of what it means to be born again and walk in all that is promised in our salvation. The Word of God is like a mirror that reflects back to us our condition, our current state of being.

God orchestrated three-day deliverance for me in Amarillo, Texas. There I quickly discovered the power of the blood of Jesus Christ. As the worship team sang "power, power, wonder-working power in the blood of the Lamb," it was then that I realized my soul – my mind, will, and emotions – were not clean. My spirit was made new, but my soul still had "bad stuff" in it. This had given the enemy legal permission to stay as long I did not choose total sanctification by God. In Thessalonians we are taught that man is a 3-part being: spirit, soul, and body. Our spirit is born again and changed when we ask Jesus to be our Savior. Our soul and body – our flesh – we are taught to yield our members completely over in surrender to God's ways and to His will and plan for our lives.

When a person comes into the light of salvation in Jesus Christ after having lived a life of sin and being abused, a true awareness that the soul needs to change happens.

Abuse leaves a deep stain of disdain. Though the spirit is made new, the old thoughts, feelings and behavior patterns still remain firmly in place. God through His Word was telling me that He was washing stain from my soul. What had been placed in me by others in secret and by what I had decided about myself was being removed by His love. It was all being replaced by His divine favor. In prayer and worship I saw myself with perfect pink pearls around my neck as I worshiped him, my beautiful slippers sparkling in His light. He so gently revealed to me, "I have been healing you and I am reassuring you of My love toward you."

The Lord then went on to say that forgiveness is the key to unlocking the door of pride over the heart and over the void in the soul. It is the very light and blood and the authority of the power of the true kingdom gospel of Christ to set a sinner, a captive, free indeed. Just as Jesus had forgiven me, I realized that it was a choice I must make to forgive others for the horrific pain and trauma.

To not forgive was to allow my personal pain to continue to drive the train of my soul, to keep me bound in compulsive behaviors of all kinds. Excessive shopping, eating disorders, sexual sin, perfectionism, performance, fears – the list was long and God wanted all of it dealt with and gone from my life. And it all must start now from a choice to walk in forgiveness.

I heard so clearly that God was telling me not to waste the opportunity to turn all that pain into a victory. That sounded strange at first, but the more I pondered it, the more clearly I saw God's desire for me to walk in total victory by His love and grace, to live above all the pain. His plan was to turn the pain into part of a great testimony of how His love conquers all and destroys every yoke of bondage. By obeying Him all the way through the healing experience and forgiving, the promise was sure to me that He would use my testimony of overcoming victory with others so they may be encouraged and healed as well. Hope is in the Lord and He nailed every abuse known to man to His wondrous cross along with all our shame, fears and disdain. It is done.

Abuse comes in many forms. I wouldn't attempt to list them all individually in this book, but I can tell you a bit about my own personal experiences. As my memory was unlocked by merciful highly trained ministers and awakened through prayer along my spiritual journey with the Lord, I became acutely aware of some specific things that had happened to me. God began to talk with me about "the Herodias effect". (Herod's plan was to kill Christ when He was a child to eliminate his competition and revival as a leader of the people of God's kingdom. Herodian's were an evil force and family.)

When I was at the very young age of two, I received a severe electric shock. I was told by my father that I had stuck a pin into an outlet and the resulting shock made me collapse. My father said he picked me up and held me. At that moment it appeared that no life was in my form. But the truth was I had been taken to be shocked, drugged and programmed.

When God began showing this to me I found myself in extreme disbelief. God led me to pray and to call my mother for confirmation of the memory. I heard the Lord tell me to bind all lies and release only the truth for pieces of my of soul's puzzle to be revealed for restoration and healing. What came out in my phone conversation with her was a shocking story of sadistic ritual abuse. My mother admitted to giving me over to eight men for a ceremony on a Druid altar at the age of 2 years. She said it happened to her and she has been dead all her life on the inside so what difference does it make. And so, I believe in God's word and have chosen to forgive my parents and grandparents by honoring the office of parent. The enemy works in darkness and in secret to bring great deception and godlessness to our minds.

In 2015 I went to Dr. Everett Cox, Deliverance Ministries, OKC, OK, for a four-hour intense prayer session. He exposed the Head Demon assigned to me as a child. The demonic force acknowledged the LIES implanted in my mind to hinder my life, i.e., I was unloved, unwanted, a failure, hated, and despised, unlovely, rejected, and hated by all. But the truth is God had given me gifts that the demon was assigned to block. The gifts are compassion, goodness, kindness, self-control, mind of Christ, giver, hospitality, beautiful tapestry, truly blessed by God, artistic, seer, evangelism, leader, prophetic, intercessor, wise, and ability to teach.

Good news. The enemy of my soul, that head demon and his friends was defeated at the cross and nailed there, rendered powerless forever.

God does heal painful memories when you are ready to face the emotional pain and go through the door of hope to reach Jesus, the Deliverer and Healer. Trust was essential for me to believe He would diffuse the pain. His love flooded my soul when by faith I chose to face the images as lies by looking on the inside of my heart with the help of highly trained, anointed prayer ministers from the Neeley Center for Health, AL and Restoration Gateway Ministries, OR.

In my experience, pieces of the mind control program would show up appearing as guardians or alters in the mind to do Satan's bidding. But God's love stood in the gap. God and His mercy called me by name and invited me to be healed of the shattering in my mind, the brokenness in my heart, and wounded soul caused by the horrific trauma.

Luke 4:18:

> *"The Spirit of the Lord is upon me, because he hath anointed me to preach the gospel to the poor; he hath sent me to heal the brokenhearted, to preach deliverance to the captives, and recovering of sight to the blind, to set at liberty them that are bruised."*

There is very definitely a divine plan, a Kingdom purpose in my living and not dying even though there were multiple attempts by the enemy to abort it.

God the Father chose my destiny before I was born.

Satan had no part in it. Sharing Jesus Christ can and will bring you across the great divide of death's abode is a great demonstration of faith in action. By an act of my will I had to choose to press in (like I was giving birth) to make it to Him as He stood on the other side. But He took the stand for me against evil men and wickedness to offer me His righteousness.

Psalm 37:3-8:

> *"3 Trust in the Lord, and do good; so shalt thou dwell in the land, and verily thou shalt be fed.*
>
> *4 Delight thyself also in the Lord; and he shall give thee the desires of thine heart.*
>
> *5 Commit thy way unto the Lord; trust also in him; and he shall bring it to pass.*
>
> *6 And he shall bring forth thy righteousness as the light, and thy judgment as the noonday.*
>
> *7 Rest in the Lord, and wait patiently for him: Fret not thyself because of him who prosper in his way, Because of the man who bring wicked devices to pass.*
>
> *8 Cease from anger, and forsake wrath: Fret not thyself in any wise to do evil."*

It was as if the scales came off my eyes and I saw color for the very first time. A veil of shame lifted off of me. I could see who God had created me to be. The change has stayed with me through all these years.

I no longer choose to believe all the lies of self-rejection, self-protection, and hatred. My life has been restored by leaps and bounds like hinds feet on high places, sure and solid. Oh, how my soul does thirst for Him. Do you realize God has a safe haven for each and every believer? You find it in Psalm 91. Read and study this over and over and see yourself in the secret place of the Most High, under the shadow of His wing.

It is essential to note here that I had to continually say yes to God as He revealed the pain and healed my soul. It was not a one-time event, but an ongoing walk with Him. I must yield to Him, to His will and direction. I prayed Psalm 51 over and over, believing Him to create a clean heart and renew a right spirit within me. Some of the memories and strongholds in my mind were very difficult and dark. But by saying yes to Him, I was being obedient, and that allowed the Holy Spirit to come into my soul with His powerful renewal and transformation. He never failed me.

I am in awe of God. We are in such serious times today. Yet I also know how His heart grieves over you and wants you as free as He has made me. He wants you to experience His love for yourself. You can be free if you want to be. It's a choice. God needs more laborers to show His love and to break down the barriers that hold back those who are dead in their trespasses, sins and emotional pain.

What of those children born and dedicated by doctors who serve Satan or nurses who dedicate newborns to the enemy before the parents even take them home from the hospital? These children don't even know what happened to them. They spend most of their lives trying to comprehend the evil strategy of the devil to thwart the plan of God for their lives. There is so much witchcraft and demonic influence all around. Evil inroads come by way of electronic media, music, and videos to mention a few. The book Dancing with Demons exposes the very root and beat of rock music originated in Africa by the hypnotic drumming of witch doctors.

Yet none of this has any power when faced with the truth of God's Word and the blood of Jesus. He was obedient to death on the cross. His blood is powerful, but we must also learn to glory in His incredible resurrection. Our focus cannot stay on the agony of His death, but must move forward into the power of His resurrection. He is no longer a babe in a manger or a suffering servant on the cross. He is raised from the dead. His dwelling place is filled with glory.

Jesus now lives in us who have accepted Him as Savior. He lives and breathes in us by the power of the Holy Spirit. Let Him indwell your heart so that you may know the good news, the power of the gospel. Choose to repent, to return this hour to know Him and His plan for your life. It is a good thing to run toward God, not away from Him! If you are driven to run away from Him, recognize the devil's hand in that; his goal is to destroy you and your seed.

It is imperative that you turn your life toward Jesus in this hour. The time is now; the door is open for you. Revelation chapter four says that God wants you to know that He loves you as much as He loves me. Know that God wants you free and Jesus gave His life so you could live free. It doesn't matter what abuses you have experienced. There are all kinds. Abuse knows no boundaries, no limits. But no matter what you may have found yourself involved in, no matter what has been done to you, there's good news. You have this book in your hands; that means you're still alive. You have hope today. Jesus hasn't forgotten you.

He is here at the door of your heart telling you that His grace is sufficient, even in the midst of the diabolical plans of the enemy to destroy you. Jesus is calling to you. You have a call – a purpose – on your life placed there by God before the foundation of the world. He is sure about you. His arm is extended to you. He's asking you to reach out simply and receive Him as the living God. Won't you choose Him in this hour? He is filled with love and grace.

Nothing you are doing in your flesh will work. You can't conjure up eternal life by any other means than through the death, burial, and resurrection of Jesus. Anything less than Him is a deception, a lie. It will not bring you life abundantly; it only leads to death. Satan is the father of lies. God is the truth, the way, and the life.

The desire of God's heart is to bring you from victim to victor, a victorious warrior for Christ. He wants you to overcome the enemy with the words of your testimony and the blood of Jesus. (Revelation 12)

Pain certainly does drive the train and all the boxcars (bondages) must be removed that produce the shattering in the mind and the wounding in the heart. Nothing is impossible for Christ. If you "park at the ark of His presence" He will meet you at your point of need. God is there with you in His thoughts. He has engraved you on the palms of

His hands. Nothing you have done, said, or experienced can keep you from His unconditional love for you. It is a choice, a decision no one can make for you. It's up to you.

It was very difficult to come out of denial and believe that the people I had trusted as a child had turned me over to the enemy. It was hard to look at their dislike for me, their own jealousy, emotional pain, and depression. It was not easy to realize what had been done to me. I have dealt with the pain of being rejected by my own mother who would have chosen to abort rather than to have another child. I've lived years being compared to my sister who was wanted.

I found out in 1998 from my father (as I blew the shofar at the family farm) that I had Jewish DNA; I was more Jewish than I would ever know. My grandfather is buried in a Jewish cemetery in Maryland. I am a Jew born anew. Amen. What does that matter? I have been to Jerusalem several times and I knew I was "home" when my feet touched the soil. Then I started seeking the Lord about whether this was true.

To confirm my father's statement, I had DNA tests done and the results should I had 1% Ashkenazi Jewish DNA markers. After intense prayer renouncing any connection with Cabbalism, God miraculously healed my DNA. I found this fascinating since DNA is directly affected by the power of Christ to be freed and in sync with heaven.

In all my trials, tribulations, sufferings, choices, losses, and ensnarement, the light of Jesus Christ has shined into my life. He has fed me rich truths until I was strong enough to be delivered unlocking the structures of programming. His timing is perfect. I encourage you to wait on the Lord. In the waiting sometimes it may seem painful and feel like you are all alone. But He does show up and He dines with you. He sends His angels to show you the way and to minister comfort to you.

If you experienced breaking of trust in your life as I did, please pray this prayer:

Lord, I know You can repair me. Teach me. I trust You, God, because I cannot trust anything else.

The deception is great, greater than anyone realizes. The godlessness in Your church has risen to Your throne. I know it grieves You. Oh, merciful God, I want to intercede and I want to lay hold of Your nail-scarred hands and pray Your will be done on earth as it is in heaven. Use me, Lord.

I want to walk and talk with You in the garden. I want to drink from your well of living water that feeds my soul. I want to smell Your fragrance and when I look at the sunrise I know You are the Creator of it all. When I look at a rainbow, I know You are there and that You care, that You know all about me. You know every hair on my head and You know my destiny and the length of my years. Oh God, reveal secrets to me as I wait on You to speak to my heart.

There is a beauty about the covenant relationship with God. It is so rich that He has woven me into the tapestry of His love toward the world. How beautiful it is to know that He is our creator, deliverer, healer, and savior. His Word testifies that He Is and testifies of His goodness toward you. When He created you He called it very good.

The enemy plants lies in our hearts and minds through painful experiences and words spoken by others in an attempt to cause us to fall away from divine destiny. From the time we are born and even after we are born again, the battle is on for our souls. We must be set free and endure with great faith till the end. Paul wrote in Ephesians 6:18-20 of the battle of the spiritual nature. Galatians chapter 5 teaches about the war of the flesh versus the spirit.

The 61st chapter of Isaiah says He gives us beauty for ashes and restores the joy. In Revelation 4, He gives us an open door to come to Him. Just knock and come in. We are really privileged and have such an inheritance in Jesus Christ. We are His beloved bride! We don't want to "waste" what Christ did on the cross for us.

Joshua made this declaration before Israel: "choose for yourselves this day that you will serve...but as for me and my house, we will serve the Lord." (Joshua 24:15) So I do not serve my past pain. I choose to serve the Lord Jesus daily; He Who has brought me to freedom and causes me to walk the holy highway of victory. I am a victor today, not a victim.

Through daily prayer I yielded and submitted to His will for me to be one with Him. He has made me His witness that He lives.

All the divine appointments, connections, and purposes He has brought into my life are to bring Him glory and honor. In His love God has opened doors of opportunity for me to be able to serve in many organizations. Through His Word He helps me to grow and mature in spiritual wisdom, understanding, knowledge and discernment. It is good to be a humble servant, a friend of God.

At one point in my walk with the Lord, I went back and looked at some photo albums of myself during my school years. When I looked into my own eyes there, I could see the pain, the melancholy of my soul. It made me thank God for those brave victorious warriors who went before me, who agreed with God's word that there truly is freedom in the power of the blood of Christ, His Word, His authority, His identity.

Oh, what a man King David was. He knew God and the power of intimacy, of worship, of relationship with Abba Father. He knew there were consequences to his choices. So he went to God and worshiped Him. David chose God's heart and His covenant and trusted in Him and in His sure mercies. God loved David for this.

As I think about the things that have happened to me either willfully or unknowingly and have overcome, I am so thankful that I am not having a pity party. I choose not to play the blame game, or fall into codependent thinking. I'm not living in the past or dwelling on the lies. I am not hopeless or powerless. Praise God that He is able to do all things exceedingly greater than I and use me in the healing process by laboring with Him.

I can share with you the hope that is in Christ Jesus. You can seize the hour, the moment, and choose a deeper walk.

There are ministers who are wounded and the enemy is waiting for his timing to bring disgrace to the kingdom of God. We need to be free. We need laborers to help others get free. We need victorious warriors. We need servants who are convinced of the God's plan to redeem the world through Jesus.

It is amazing that our mind, will, and emotions can be so bound, programmed by the enemy. Our belief system should be aligned with the promises and word of God. Familiarity, intellectualism, humanism, and compromise blind us from knowing we are deceived. Ask yourself if you are you walking in His power or your own soul power?

In the darkest hour when you think you will perish, God will reveal to you in your inner spirit how much He loves you and that His banner over you is love. Open up your ears and eyes to know He is God. The counterfeit looks pretty real sometimes. It can do miracles, signs, wonders and make you look pretty spiritual. But when you become a minister of fire, and the life of Jesus burns within you, then you know that you know that He knows you and you are experiencing God as a burning bush.

Please pray with me and allow the Holy Spirit to move like a fresh wind to blow through you.

If you have never received Christ as your Savior, would you receive healing, deliverance, the baptism of Holy Spirit and fire? Do you have pain in your heart? If you are in need in any area of your life, let your mind be touched. Let strongholds come down. If you have believed lies and false teachings, let the light of Jesus Christ shine in the darkness of your mind and let the true Shepherd come and speak truth to you so that you may be set free of the mind-binding spirits of fear, anxiety, depression, oppression, heaviness, suicide, addictions of all kinds, and trauma. Let God speak to you that you will know with great confidence that He is the resurrected Savior seeking to save your soul this hour.

CHAPTER 1:

Jesus Christ the Healer

This is a personal invitation to join God on a great adventure to face the darkness of the soul. God wants to make a divine exchange to transform your heart through His liquid love released over you. This great adventure can be summed up in one: Jesus Christ. Jesus has come to heal your broken, bruised heart.

Picture, if you will, the three nails driven into the hands and feet of Jesus Christ, the ultimate warrior and lone survivor. The sign over his head read "King of the Jews". In your mind's eye see those nails bearing these labels on them: Divine Compassion, Divine Humility, and Divine Servant-hood. And as you view this picture of Jesus at Calvary, also know this truth: this same Jesus took all your sin nature – all your emotional pain, survivor's guilt, rejection, soul wounds, heartache, loss, pride, abuses, disdain, fears, shame everything you've ever done wrong and ever will – and nailed it to the cross for you. He is letting you know that it is all forgiven, washed by His blood forever and ever. God is greater than your sin or pain.

Jesus Himself said in John 8:31-32:

> *"31...If ye continue in my word, then are you my disciples indeed; 32 And you shall know the truth, and the truth shall make you free."*

The realm of the soul (the mind, will and emotions) is where Satan deceives us. In Colossians 2:8 we, as believers, are told:

> *" See to it that no one takes you captive through hollow and deceptive philosophy, which depends on human tradition and the elemental spiritual forces[a] of this world rather than on Christ."*

According to this scripture, there are really just two game plans or strategies to follow:

1. **A hollow and deceptive philosophy based on human tradition and religion.**
2. **Teachings built on Christ's unconditional love for you in a personal relationship.**

What is a hollow and deceptive philosophy? Something that is hollow has no center. It appears solid, but is not. If Jesus is not at the center of your life with peace, you are falling for hollow deception. Satan has not changed his base of operation since the beginning. He is still telling the same two lies. Jesus gave you the keys to His Escape plan.

Victim or a Warrior Shining in the darkness as a Star

In this world in which we live today, it is reported that approximately one out of five men and women has been abused by an adult or family member by the age of eighteen. We struggle to understand or believe statistics like that, especially if most of our friends and acquaintances are Christians. But the numbers indicate otherwise. Sexual, physical or spiritual abuse knows no religious, social, or economic boundaries. And until it happens to you don't know how it feels.

Abuse brings a deadening to the soul of the victim. The secret lament of the soul damaged by abuse must be gently explored in order to lay hold of the new hope buried there. Where is that one to go when thirsty and dry? God invites the hurting one to come to the river flowing from His throne and be washed clean of all that stain of shame, deep pain of loss, deferred hope and the undeniable fear that it will happen again.

It is God's will today for you, the wounded survivor of abuse, to come to the Great Physician for healing. It is time to start your healing process, to continue if you've already begun. What a great blessing to become a compassionate player in someone else's healing journey, too.

Jesus wants to take you on an unforgettable journey of scriptural resolution, and power of the Holy Spirit's anointing in God's path of healing. What may seem difficult in the beginning addressing the memories of that moment in time but Jesus is there as you open the door of hope and faiths to have Him heal the memories which will lead to a life characterized by His unconditional love.

Are you in need of healing of memories, healing of emotions, healing of the past, making peace with the past, searching for significance, and desiring Godly counsel? How do all of these play a part in the restoration of a Christian? Can a traumatized or distressed one be made truly whole? Recognizing that you may have a "dead" soul may seem daunting. It's a bit like looking up at the night sky filled with stars and hoping to see a glimmer of light – a door of hope – someone to light the way out of the confusion and emptiness. Breaking cycle of unbelief and choosing faith is very exciting choice full of wonder and amazement.

A shattered soul, splintered mind, and broken heart laid so bare by abuse create a driven, compulsive, or restless wandering soul in the victim. For example, I personally had to excel and be the very best in my career or I was compelled to travel, or move around a lot to see what was on the other side never content or at peace with me. This causes one to be willing to go to great lengths to find fulfillment from the world. Alas, fulfillment for the flesh to be satisfied is an impossible and fruitless goal. *"Seek first the Kingdom of God and His righteousness"*... is a focus point or a goal to pursue to stop the wanderings, Matthew 6:33.

The love of Jesus Christ is the only way of escape from this chaotic hurtful place. In Him it is possible to leave the wilderness mentality behind. Only Jesus can take that pain and turn it into joy. Read Isaiah 61 and Luke 4:18 and it becomes very clear that Jesus came to set the captives free. Realizing and admitting you are a captive or slave to deception of this world is a good place to be. King David discovered this truth when he wrote this Psalm and made it a prayer to God.

> *"Create in me a clean heart, O God; and renew a right spirit within me." – Psalm 51:10*

What is contained within the wounded heart? Just to start with you will discover there is usually much hopelessness, powerlessness, pain, confusion, chaos and distress. Often the individual has lost their ability to trust. One is not sure whether or not to love or to receive love. And how to even begin to recognize you may have never known holy, pure, unconditional love in your life. Conditional love leaves one questioning "What is love?" Unfortunately, the wounding can also give way to evil thoughts and beliefs that do not align themselves with the truth of God's Word. Therein lays the choice of the will to believe God's word over what you have been taught or familiar things you have learned.

Evil avoids light at all cost. It feeds on subtlety. It rejoices in death and despises the legitimate satisfaction of the soul. This shunning of God and running away from Him is the very opposite of what this heart needs to do. God wants His children to run to Him when they have troubles, not to hide themselves away from Him. There is really no way to truly hide from Him; He is everywhere and He is love. He will bring the prodigals, the wounded, and the backslidden home to the Father's heart. I could not imagine seeking the Father's love because my earthly father was not there to hold me, protect me, rock me or sit me on his lap. When I saw a child being loved by the father, jealousy rose up in me and the hurt/longing of what I never experienced as a child, my child heart wept over the loss.

The effects of abuse must yield to the quest for a cure or answers to injustices. These dynamics are the reality of spiritual war. It becomes part of the abused one's armor of self-defense and protection to deflect the pain by avoiding or confronting memories of the traumatic event. The clash and wrestling with contempt becomes the war zone. The scars of abuse lie sometimes quietly, but always alive within: powerlessness, helplessness, hopelessness, shame, betrayal, and ambivalence. These breed other secondary symptoms and deeply affect all other relationships. The battle must be faced; Satan and his strategies of lies which are targeting the wounded soul. God is faithful to lift the veil of shame from your face so His glory can shine through and bring down the stronghold of lies in what you believe about God, self and others. The Holy Spirit is faithful to reveal these lies one by one as you by faith replace them with God's truth.

It may seem an unlikely route to freedom, love, and joy, but it all begins with honesty, an open heart, forgiveness, true repentance and brokenness, and humility. Confrontation of the pain and the wounds within brings restoration and sets the soul free to soar through the damaged emotions.

How does God heal your wounded heart? He is faithful and true to His Word. He will love you into trust and obedience without a shadow of doubt He is able.

Psalm 23:

> "1 *The Lord is my shepherd; I shall not want.*
>
> 2 *He makes me to lie down in green pastures: He leads me beside the still waters.*
>
> 3 *He restores my soul: He leads me in the paths of righteousness for his name's sake.*
>
> 4 *Yea, though I walk through the valley of the shadow of death, I will fear no evil: for thou art with me; thy rod and thy staff they comfort me.*
>
> 5 *Thou prepare a table before me in the presence of mine enemies: thou anoint my head with oil; my cup runs over.*

> [6] *Surely goodness and mercy shall follow me all the days of my life: and I will dwell in the house of the Lord forever."*

This scripture is sure and is our promise from our loving Father that goodness and mercy will be with us to the end of our days.

Luke 4:18:

> *"The Spirit of the Lord is upon me, because he hath anointed me to preach the gospel to the poor; he hath sent me to heal the brokenhearted, to preach deliverance to the captives, and recovering of sight to the blind, to set at liberty them that are bruised."*

Hebrews 11:30:

> *"By faith the walls of Jericho fell down, after they were compassed about seven days."*

The children of Israel had to walk in faith as they were obedient to do what the Lord told them outside the great walled city of Jericho before the walls fell down. It must have seemed an impossible thing to them as they marched each time around those high walls. But this scripture clearly states that because of their faith those huge impossible walls came down. When I said yes to a divine appointment to go and receive at a Women's Aglow meeting, God orchestrated for my cinder-block wall of self-protection to fall under His presence. This same faith that resides in you and that comes to you by hearing the Word of God (Romans 10:17) is the victory that overcomes the mountains of pain hidden deep within. In Exodus the children of Israel believed following Moses by walking on sand as the waters parted at the Red Sea. Moses gave the command and he lifted up his staff obeying and trusting God to save them from the Pharaohs army who were in hot pursuit. The waters engulfed the enemy destroying the Egyptians. The Israelites crossed over to freedom. This is power and authority we have as we stand in Christ and allow Him to fight for us and let the water of God's word defend us.

In Hebrews 12:1 we are admonished to,

> *"Lay aside every weight, and the sin which doth so easily beset us, and let us run with patience the race that is set before us".*

Part of the race for those who have been abused is daring to be vulnerable to the Holy Spirit in order to release all the poison that seeps into the soul as a result of the trauma endured. Healing is accomplished in Christ Jesus and we receive it through His love for us in intimate prayer/communion and personal ministry.

A huge element of receiving healing, centers on the imperative fact that we must forgive the taker, user, predator, and abuser. Forgiveness does not in any way justify their actions or say that it is okay for them to have violated our will as they did. True forgiveness disentangles us from the abuser and releases them to God. Scripture gives us some definitive truth on the subject:

Hebrews 12:14-15:

> *"14 Follow peace with all men, and holiness, without which no man shall see the Lord: 15 looking diligently lest any man fail of the grace of God; lest any root of bitterness springing up trouble you, and thereby many are defiled;"*

One requirement for receiving healing of the heart is to choose to believe that the blame game is over. The habit of blaming someone else must be laid down. The accuser loves to point the finger away from itself transferring attention and guilt to another, never willing to look in the mirror of self. As we peer into our own self, however, and look on the inside, it is then and only then that we are taken back by the reality of all the lies the enemy of our soul has convinced us to be true about ourselves. This strategy blocks the gifts and callings that were granted before you were born. Upon this revelation of truth and exposure, a new belief to trust in a living and loving God emerges as the lies about God are exposed by the truth of His word by choosing to have Satan lies defeated and establishing God as the victor. God wants to restore your heart, your mind, your soul so you can live abundantly and reflect His glory through your life. His desire is for you to be a witness of His grace, to walk in faith, and experience Him performing His Word through you.

The love of God is a bold, unconditional (agape) love. You quickly understand that God's love operating in us and through us calls for us to be selfless, just as Jesus was selfless in all He did. The benefits of learning to walk in the love of God are boundless and eternal.

1 Corinthians 13:4-8

> *"4 Charity suffers long, and is kind; charity envies not; charity vaunted not itself, is not puffed up, 5 doth not behave itself unseemly, seeks not her own, is not easily provoked, thinks no evil; 6 rejoices not in iniquity, but rejoices in the truth; 7 bears all things, believeth all things, hopes all things, endures all things. 8 Charity never fails: but whether there are prophecies, they shall fail; whether there are tongues, they shall cease; whether there is knowledge, it shall vanish away."*

Dying to Self

Forgiveness and trust in the love of God are necessary parts of healing especially when you have been forgotten or neglected or purposely set at naught. In all abuse situations there does come the feelings of insult or oversight. When our words are twisted, our opinion disregarded and ridiculed...these are times to lean on God's kind of love. These are the times when we choose to walk in love and not allow the desire to seek self-justification or revenge. Instead, we call forth the love of God within, and trusting in His love, we don't consider the suffered wrongs that come our way. We get genuinely happy when others succeed and we rejoice with them without envy. With this kind of love we are able to put others before ourselves always. And this love never fails – others or us. Ask for God's radical love to penetrate you heart.

When we are forgotten or neglected or purposely set at naught, yet we don't sting or hurt with the insult or the oversight, but our heart is happy being counted worthy to share in Christ's suffering – that is dying to self. Maybe our words are twisted, our opinions and advice ridiculed. When we can refuse to let anger even rage rise in our heart or even defend ourselves, but take it all in stride with patience, gentleness and self-control – that is dying to self. When we patiently bear annoyances and grievances and any and all of the things that distress us or aggravate us in life without reacting, blowing up over it – that is dying to self.

Dying to self, or putting others first before ourselves, has virtually no limits. We are constantly faced with circumstances and situations that challenge us to either walk in love or seek our own way. Sometimes it may be in the simplest things like having to eat food that we don't care for or the climate not being what we want or our expectations not met. Perhaps we get to interact with people who are difficult to be around or who believe differently than we do. Love of the God-kind will always think the best of the other person and humbly endure any discomfort for love's sake.

How do we know when we've died to ourselves? We become a new creature in Christ at salvation, the old man dies and the new man arises. However, sanctification is a process, but when we stop wanting to constantly refer to ourselves in conversation or to record our own good works and words, when we cease itching after commendations, when we truly prefer to be unknown – that is dying to self. When we can see our brother prosper and have his needs met and honestly rejoice with him, feeling no envy, no questioning God while your own need seems to be unmet at the time – that is dying to self. When we can receive correction and humbly submit inwardly as well as outwardly without our heart filling with rebellion or resentment – that is dying to self. Our child heart will scream for its way always. I want, I need this and this.

So, are you dead yet? In these last days, the Spirit will bring us to the cross. In Philippians 3:10 (NKJV) we hear the cry of Paul's heart:

"...That I may know Him and the power of His resurrection, and the fellowship of His sufferings, being conformed to His death."

It is true that He has forgiven us for all our sins. Everything we experience must be nailed to the cross. How many of this list of issues do you feel you still need to deal with at the cross with Jesus?

- Forgiving yourself and others
- Searching for significance
- Attempting to meet your own needs
- Fear of failing—"I have to be perfect"
- The Performance trap—"I have to perform correctly in order to be loved"
- Fear of rejection—"I am an approval addict"
- Shame—"I am what I am"
- Guilt—"I play the blame game and I'm unworthy to be loved"

All these were dealt with by Jesus when He was on the cross for you. Because of the cross you have in Him the grace, the ability to:

- Forgive yourself and others
- Find your significance in His love, not by your own works
- Have all your needs met according to His riches in glory in Christ
- Know that God is always with you, therefore, you do not have to "be perfect"
- Know that you are justified, forgiven, and pleasing to God, not based on your performance, but on His love
- Know you are reconciled to God and accepted by Him, therefore you are free to love others without depending on their approval of you
- Know you are complete in Christ and shame is taken away from you. What you are is a new creation in Him. All the old is passed away.

- Know you are deeply love by God and free to walk away from the need to be punished.

Yes, the trip to the cross of Calvary is a life-changing experience. His blood cleanses you and makes you white as snow. It makes you righteous before a holy God of love. We can place the cross between us and break the power of the law of sowing and reaping for every judgment we have spoken. Amazing power is in the cross and we are just discovering the depth of what was done by Christ.

Our walk with the Lord Jesus Christ is not something we only do at church or at certain times, but it is a moment-by-moment ongoing relationship with Him. The healing of our mind – the Bible refers to it as the renewing of our mind – is a process of replacing our old ungodly thoughts and beliefs with the truth of God's Word. We must become aware of what we are thinking and believing, and then replace those that are inconsistent with what God says. Word curses spoken by others can literally control your mind if you let them, i.e., "You are ugly, You are crazy, You are unworthy, You are unclean, You will never amount to anything, You are mine, I hate you, You should never have been born, You should never been born, You are a mistake, You can't do anything right, You are a waste of time, You are too difficult, I wanted a boy not a girl, You are a loser, You are not very smart, You are a failure."

The beginning of this process is to first ask the Holy Spirit to reveal to us those familiar thoughts and beliefs that we take as truth, but do not really measure up to the plumb line of God's word. You can often begin by asking some basic questions.

One might be, "What lie do I believe that is controlling my behavior, emotions, or actions?" For example, do I believe I am unworthy? Unclean? No self-control? I'll never change? I'll always be fat? I'm unattractive? Inferior? Do you say things to yourself like, "If I was a really good person I would be able to control my eating"?

We can be truly hard on ourselves and this is clearly not God's view or opinion of us. God loved us so much He sent Jesus to bring us back to abundant life. John 3:16 tells us so. The answer to all those internal thoughts, questions and self-comments above is, "I am who Jesus says I am." Someone once said they asked God how much He loves us and

He stretched out His arms on the cross and said, "I love you this much and more."

He really does love us more than we can comprehend. There is a victim/victory cycle which takes us to a point of decision when it comes to temptation and doing the same behavior over and over while expecting a change. This is defined as insanity. If we choose sin, we are the devil's captive through willful disobedience. This choice brings heaviness upon the soul, sometimes depression and oppression. If we choose a life of faith and resist the temptation, we walk in joy and bear the fruit of the Spirit: love, joy, peace, goodness, kindness, meekness, patience and self-control.

It is a lie that tempts us to disobey and sin. The only way to escape the lie is to take it captive and replace it with God's truth about ourselves, others, and our own situation. To resist that lie is to stand strong in our faith. How wonderful it is, though, that if we do fall into that sin, there is still love and hope for us. By confessing our sin, repenting, receiving His forgiveness and forgiving ourselves restoration comes to your soul – now that is real power.

We can count on Him to make the crooked ways straight. God does care. He is there. He does know about us. He is in control for He is sovereign covenant keeping God.

Matthew 6:33:

> *"But seek ye first the kingdom of God, and his righteousness; and all these things shall be added unto you."*

What a message of hope and encouragement this is. God has given us many scriptures to help us stay true to Him and resist the temptations around us. Some of them are below:

1 John 4:4:

> *"You are of God, little children, and have overcome them, because He who is in you is greater than he who is in the world."*

Philippians 4:13:

"I can do all things through Christ which strengthens me." Romans 8:1:

"There is therefore now no condemnation to them which are in Christ Jesus, who walk not after the flesh, but after the Spirit."

Psalm 118:1:

"O give thanks unto the Lord; for he is good: because his mercy endures forever."

"Greater is He who is in me than he who is in the world." – 1 John 4:4

God has given us His way to be free or remain in bondage. The book of Ephesians teaches how to walk as a Christian with divine character. Galatians gives us grace and reminds us not to be bewitched by false teaching. The pathway is clear: **follow a real relationship with Jesus.**

In Revelation 21:9 we hear an angel speak,

"Come, I will show you the bride, the Lamb's wife."

God is calling and gathering His bride, for behold, He comes to have a great adventure of the heart. He wants a love reformation in us and He wants it to spread throughout the heart of His creation. We as believers are called to be His bride.

In order to be a part of His love revolution, there are basic things we need to have put in order in our lives. The most essential and most obvious is for us to be born again and filled with the Holy Spirit's fire. We then can spiritually mature in Him, repenting when needful and letting go of any offenses. We take up our cross daily and follow Him in service using our spiritual gifts. It is true that many of you have done this, but have you opened your heart to allow God to lead you to minister one-on-one to others in prayer, disciple or deliverance?

Hurting people do hurt people. How are we to react when our feelings are hurt? What is our first response? We are to respond acting Christ like in God's love – taking no notice of a suffered wrong. Responding by a reaction with rejection of the person, a critical tongue toward them, an air of judgment against them, withdrawal from them – all these only serve to damage or lose the relationship. That is not love but emotional escapism or insulation.

If we are to move into the fullness of heart healing, we must be directed to the place where we recognize in the hurting and hurtfulness of others their true need for the Lord. Everyone wants to be loved and fear not being loved. They need His compassion, His mercy. They need Jesus. We must stay in the love of God that will reach out to them and, being led by the Spirit, pray for them, minister to them, love them. Many times our testimony will become a very powerful tool in helping someone else realize there is hope for them, too, just like there was for us. Regardless of their circumstances, they will learn through your love, faith and experiences that God's way of restoration is very clear and present day reality.

A real birthing of the great love revolution in the body of Christ is happening. Jews are being saved in Israel. Believers are being birthed all over the globe. By faith we lay hold of what only God can do and will do in our lives. In Revelation 19:7 (NKJV) we read,

> *"Let us be glad and rejoice and give Him glory, for the marriage of the Lamb has come, and His wife has made herself ready."*

We are to live our lives rooted in Jesus' love for others.

This is so very exciting. He wants to speak to us, to marry us. He wants to love us...you...like we have never experienced before. He wants to share intimately with us His desires, dreams and visions for us. Won't you come on this great adventure with Him? This invitation requires an

RSVP. Will you receive from Him great insights and revelation into His coming, to be ready as a bride would adorn herself for the bridegroom?

He is calling us to come up higher, to know Him more intimately as the days and years go by and our entrance into eternity draws closer. He will make His mysteries and secrets known to us. What is the cry of the bridegroom? "Come."

Are you a settled Christian? Will you choose to receive from the fountain of life, living waters? What is the fragrance? Could it be myrrh and frankincense? Ask yourself: What awaits me if I surrender my will and say, "Yes, Lord, yes."? Have the little foxes robbed me of my joy? My strength? My vision? My time with You, Lord? Your glory? Do I see myself as a lily among the brambles? Have I come outside my wall of self-protection and defense? Have I waited too long to spend time in communion with Him? What is keeping me outside?

We must search our hearts, each of us, to know where we stand with Him. Am I truly devoted to Him? Do I beg Him to remove all burdens, care and worries from me? Am I using the keys to the kingdom that He sacrificially gave on the cross so I could be free to bind the word to my heart and loose myself from this world? It is so easy for us as believers to go soft on sin, to allow things in our lives that do not bring glory and honor to His name.

We know that God will not be mocked; He will not be manipulated. He will not meet our demands. He will not surrender to our wills, to our selfish desires. He will not step outside of His perfect timing and plan of redemption.

Our prayers should ultimately change us in His presence. We must accept that without the blood of Jesus washing us clean and making us new, our best efforts in our flesh are as filthy rags. Without Him we have not arrived. We are to walk in humble obedience before our God and worship Him in Spirit and in Truth. He is worthy of our praise. He is worthy of our daily worship.

It must become a continual daily quest to ask, seek, knock and find God's will for us, walking in love before Him, repenting and receiving His forgiveness when we fall to temptation.

Life Savers

1. True salvation

Our Father Who art in Heaven, hallowed by thy name. Can you say with me?

He has adopted me into His kingdom. I proclaim that, because of Christ's redemption, I am a new creation of infinite worth. I am deeply loved. I am completely forgiven. I am fully pleasing. I am totally accepted by God. I am absolutely complete in Christ. Therefore, there has never been another person like me in the history of mankind, nor will there ever be. God has made me an original. I am one of a kind. He has made me to be a real somebody.

2. Direction

The cry of your heart must be: Thy kingdom come; thy will be done on earth as it is in heaven.

- Are you ready?
- Are you preparing, equipping, and training?
- Is your heart Christ's home?
- Does rebellion or pride have any place in your attitudes or actions?
- Do you choose to adopt a submissive spirit?
- Have you repented for areas of your life you have kept independent from obedience to God?

3. Words contain power

Life and death are in the power of the tongue. Our words are very important. Proverbs 9:13 (AMP) tells us that,

> *"The foolish woman is noisy; she is simple and open to all forms of evil, she [willfully and recklessly] knows nothing whatever [of eternal value]."*

We must set a guard over our mouth to keep watch over the door of our lips (Psalm 141:3). Can you picture yourself with His holiness now? What would come out of your mouth? We will be married to Jesus. Your earthly marriage is a training ground for your heavenly one with Him, a marriage without regrets.

Amos 3:3 teaches us that two cannot walk together unless they make an appointment and agree. Ask the Holy Spirit by His power to help you overcome the urge to speak before God tells you to. Ask Him to be a guard at your lips. Please stay in agreement with Him as to what to speak and when and to whom

4. He is our source

Let all your needs be met through our loving Father God. It delights Him when we come to Him in trust to meet our every need. It is His joy and pleasure to take care of us as we come in simple faith. It brings Him no glory or honor for us to look to ourselves or outside influences for our help. "Give us this day our daily bread..." This is worship. Are you seeking Him for today's nourishment? The word of God should be honey to our lips.

We worship God:

- To show He is worthy of our intimacy. He is the only One Who can fulfill our need and bring us to selflessness.
- To receive His love and to give His love. We love because He first loved us (1 John 4:19).
- To take on His well-being within our heart, soul, and mind (Matthew 6:25-26, 28-33).
- To feel secure in our Abba Father, our papa. He guarantees your personal security. (Galatians 4:6).
- To experience His approval. Let your ears hear the blessing of "Well done my good and faithful servant" (Matthew 25:20).
- To bask in His unconditional love that accepts us totally. In Him we are worthy, clean, whole, valuable, and precious.

5. Forgiveness

Forgiveness is a choice. God expects us to forgive in order to walk in His love and in the fullness of His Spirit. We are to forgive just as Jesus did and does. We cannot accomplish this in our own strength. Forgiving someone is not saying that what they did to hurt us was okay. Forgiving them is not really about them at all. It is much more about our choosing to release them, thus enabling us to walk free of the tentacles of pain and bitterness that try mightily to keep us from the Love walk and true healing and freedom. Let the Holy Spirit shine His light into your mind as you pray this prayer.

If you need to forgive someone and let them go so you can move on in your walk with God, please pray this prayer:

Father, when <u>(say the person's name who hurt you)</u> did <u>(say what they did that hurt you)</u> to me, it hurt me. It <u>(express how it affected you)</u>. But now in obedience to Your divine Will for my life, I choose to forgive <u>(person's name)</u> for doing this and for hurting me in this way. I choose to let all the anger, bitterness, and hatred, all the hurt within me go. I give it to You, Lord, and I thank You that I walk free of it now by faith, in the name of Jesus. Thank you that I am free of unforgiveness. I am now free to love and heal and move on in my relationship with you.

6. Vigilance

Be mindful to keep your will surrendered/yielded to the Father's will. Watch that you do not put up walls to keep God out of areas of your heart and life. Submission is an offensive weapon. Keeping a guard on your lips and watchfulness to your heart will help you remain ready at all times for whatever may come your way. Be a sharp listener for the voice of the Holy Spirit as He gives you unction – to pray, to speak, to forgive, to repent. Be quick to obey His softest word. Indifference is an enemy of our faith. Paul wrote to Timothy in 2 Timothy 3:1 that we are living in perilous times – harsh, savage times abounding in vices, barren of virtue. We are to guard our hearts continually to keep ourselves from the relentless enemy crouching always nearby. Him we are to resist by submitting ourselves to God and obeying Him.

7. Prayer

Are you spending time in prayer daily? This is something that we see Jesus doing as part of His daily life. We must take time to draw aside as He did in order to hear what our Father is saying to us, in order for us to see what He would have us do. When doubts and fears and questions come, we must have the habit of taking our confusion to Him and allowing Him to clarify all things for us. Nothing is impossible with God. Trust Him in prayer to bring down any walls that need to fall. He will shine His holy light in the darkness of your mind and reveal what you need to see and to know.

8. Ministry of the Holy Spirit

Oh, the ministry of the Holy Spirit is an awesome experience. How I love it. He is God's very own agent on the earth sent to fulfill the new covenant in us. He shows no partiality. He will give gifts to you as you seek Him, as you give your life to serve Him. Spend time with Him daily. Become aware of His presence with you and in you all the time. He resides within you to lead and guide you into all truth.

CHAPTER 2:

Men and Women of Honor

Men and women are blessed by God and have a definite role to play, not only in creation of the next generation, but in being the heart of the home, the center of life. Many women are multi-talented and diverse, therefore, they multi-task effortlessly. Men are goal oriented, project centered, providers and protectors of their families normally.

The adult women in my life were all exceptional women and great examples of being strong and faithful. Without a mate by their side to support them financially or emotionally, they managed to feed, clothe, and care for a household of ten people. I watched my grandmother manage her money down to the penny, using Green Stamps to get those extra things for the home. Both my mother and her sister returned to school to learn secretarial skills in order to provide for their children. They were all strong women of character and integrity.

My grandfather was the provider until he passed when I was 8 years old which created a void in the home and the running of the household was left to the three women and six children.

I grew up with a complex role model dominated by three strong women: my grandmother, mother who had three children and aunt who had three children for a total of nine people. They met their obligations toward their children by working to provide food and clothing. My grandmother did her Christian duty to stay home preparing meals and security but it was not normal order according to God's biblical plan for marriage and household.

The idea, let alone the reality, of a normal, healthy Christian marriage and family has changed dramatically. This has given way to some confusion for the male and female roles today. Abusive, broken marriages and relationships abound. Are we destined to continue the downward spiral or is there a better way? Can we come to understand and fall in line with God's ways? What does the man and woman of honor and integrity "look like" today? Where are we in developing Godly character in the next generations?

In Genesis 3, God created both male and female-two separate and defined sexes and called them male and female "very good." Male and female He created those who were to take dominion and authority over the earth. But in my growing-up years, we very much lacked a male figure to balance out the picture of God's design for a mother/father head of the home. This required a deep and powerful renewing of my mind – exchanging the lies I believed to be true for God's truth. Imagine three adult women in charge and six children all trying to grasp the reality of God's divine order.

One of the works Jesus did was bring freedom to men and women, freedom from the bondages of abuse, misplaced authority, false judgment, intimidation, and domination. Countless people respond to Christ's teachings because of the freedom and acceptance He brought. His truth was opposite the trends and perceptions of the day then; the same remains true today. A woman is not sub-human, but co-equal with a man and is meant to rule and reign with man, taking dominion in the earth.

We see Mary at Jesus' feet in Luke 14:25 learning by being respecting the Rabbani's teachings. We see the woman who was to be stoned gets delivered. We see women in the upper room in Acts 1:8 as the majority waiting for the Holy Spirit. We see the woman bent over in Luke weighed down with false burdens put on her by religious leaders in a male-dominated society and religion.

As a woman of God, when I was gathered with other women to pray in my home, I saw the banqueting table of the Lord with a chair just for me. He invited me to sit down with the other men and women. I was not disqualified by my gender, but embraced for my love and obedience to the Lord.

Another time in prayer Jesus opened my eyes to see His nail-scarred hands reaching to me to take hold of them and agree with Him for intercession. Christ has so blessed me with His love, affection, and prayers that I know He knows me and I choose to know Him more and more. During a moment of deep fellowship with God when deep wounds were healed, He came and sat at the table with me and comforted me. I have found that Christ will always show the way if I follow His will. The Holy Spirit has no gender issues, for He is preparing the Bride for the Bridegroom.

He is a just and righteous God who chose me to serve Him as a witness (Isaiah 43) and minister to Him. His love, acceptance, security, and promises fulfilled the voids in my heart. It is amazing to seek Him and to experience this mystery of faith. By making the choice to be fulfilled in Him I have discovered myself – my gifts, talents, and abilities designed from creation to glorify the Messiah, Christ my Lord and Savior. Being tuned in to His voice and obeying Him brings great peace to the soul.

He has chosen you, too, and desires for you to take the journey of discovery of whom He made you to be. Let Him transform you; the Father knows best; He wrote the manual, the Bible. Honor and Integrity

It is important to look at the eight characteristics of honor and integrity, a person of excellence, diligence and honesty. In most of my travels and daily life, people who have allowed Christ to mold them into His image and allowed God to develop their character share these eight basic qualities.

1. **Honesty. The truth will set you free from any lie. Do not allow deception to blind you. If you don't know the answer to something, don't talk about it. Don't hide behind pride.**

2. **Humility. Promote the gospel of Christ with power. (James 4:10)**
3. **Obedience. It is a choice every hour every day to obey. (Psalm 40:8) God will not make you do anything against your will, but peace does come when you are obedient.**
4. **Merciful. He gives you a heart for the hurting with compassion to reach out to them. Let Christ heal through you. Let the Holy Spirit teach you. (Matthew 5:7)**
5. **Gentleness. The Holy Spirit will move and speak to your heart just the right thing to say at the right time. Just ask! (1 Peter 3:3-4)**
6. **Wisdom. Pray for it and ask for the knowledge of wisdom and discretion. (James 3:3)**
7. **Surrender and stand (for those who are married). Marriage is meant to be a "forever" relationship. Watch to not get out of order. Keep your priorities straight. (Galatians 2:20) If you are single, Christ becomes your husband as you yield and submit to Him.**
8. **Love. Love at all times, even the enemy. In the face of every offense that comes at you, treat it as another opportunity to walk in love in order to win them to the Lord.**

For those who are married, the following are very helpful keys for standing by your mate:

1. **Unconditional love. Accept him as he is. Changing him is God's job; praying for him is yours.**
2. **Be an encourager. (1 Thessalonians 5:11) He will love it. It's part of a man's design; it's in their DNA. It means so much to be affirmed.**
3. **Communicate. Talk to him and with him, not at him. Tell him how you feel. Avoid using "you" statements. For example, instead of saying, "You hurt my feelings when you yelled at me," you can say, "When I heard your voice raised in anger at me I felt like you didn't love me." He is less likely to become defensive when you speak this way**

because you won't be attacking him, even if you felt like he attacked you.

4. **Respect & submission (divine order). Doing things God's way brings blessings. Understanding a man's emotions and letting him know it is okay and safe to cry helps him to release his feelings. God has ordained the husband to be a covering for the wife because of the blessings of God's covenant.**

I read a book called 10 Lies the Church Tells Women by Lee Grady. In it the author explains a great deal of what has been taught in the church for hundreds of years against women in authority, women gender, lies about women's state of mind and emotions, etc. Men have propagated these lies as well. Here are the basic ten:

1. **God created women as inferior being destined to serve their husbands.**
2. **Women are not equipped to assume leadership roles in the church.**
3. **Women must not teach or preach to men in a church setting.**
4. **A woman should view her husband as the "priest" of the home.**
5. **A man needs to "cover" a woman in her ministry activities.**
6. **Women who exhibit strong leadership qualities pose a serious danger to the church.**
7. **Women are more easily deceived than men.**
8. **Women can't be fulfilled or spiritually effective without a husband**
9. **Women shouldn't work outside the home.**
10. **Women must obediently submit to their husbands in all situations.**

In each of these points the direct opposite is the truth. Walking in humility and obedience to the Lord's will does not have a gender attached to it.

If you were Satan, what better strategy is there in order to win the end time battle than to cut your opposition in half by spinning lies to eliminate and intimidate half of God's glorious end time army?

Have you ever asked the questions, "Who am I as a woman? What is my identity? What are my attributes?" When you look into the mirror who do you see? What do you like about yourself? These are powerful questions that are worthy of your time and attention in order to better see yourself the way God sees you.

We must come to see ourselves fresh and new in Him. It is important to take a good look at who God created you to be. Write down your positive characteristics and physical features. Then write down the negative ones or those that you are not happy with and begin a plan of transformation.

As a great exercise for yourself, go to a mirror and begin to speak to her as one whom God created. Look yourself in the eye and say, "You're God's favorite, a princess. God loves you. I can wear anything and look good. I am gifted, anointed and blessed. I am God's beloved."

You will be amazed at how much this will help you see yourself differently. Begin to develop who you are. Learn to minister to others out of that. Allow yourself to be who God created to you be.

I believe God has called us out and protected us for such a time as this. Don't waste any more time! Let's begin to take steps to bring change by renewing the mind and setting goals to bring us closer to Him. It's helpful to spend time around other successful women who can encourage us in our journey.

In contrast to the woman of integrity, the following describes a woman who is split with rebellion and rejection, needing the Master's loving nature to be healed and renewed. Notice the huge differences:

1. **Unable to establish healthy relationships.**
2. **Creates issues; lives in a constant storm.**
3. **Is difficult and draining to be around.**
4. **Unable to be stable in a marriage relationship.**

5. **Will not submit to authority.**
6. **Unable to make a choice and stick with it.**
7. **Always in conflict with other people.**
8. **Sometimes manifests wide personality or emotional swings**
9. **Revelation of hands diagram is a network of demons**

Have you ever heard it said, "I would change if I knew how, but since I don't know what to do, I guess I won't?" Well, God is the answer – the source – and He is the one who changes people when they seek Him for it.

The key is simply this: Surrendering to Jesus Christ as your Lord and Savior is the healing balm you are seeking. Release it all and lay it all down at His feet – your pain, your guilt, your wounded heart, and all your emotional, mental, and physical needs. Jesus is truly the transformer.

CHAPTER 3:

You Have a Voice — Use It

Most victims of abuse and trauma to include mental distress and vexations of the mind are reluctant to speak out on important issues or have the boldness to share the gospel of Jesus Christ. A "spirit of silence" (out of being threatened by their predator) besets the abused one. Most are fearful to use their voice and some are terrified of standing up for something they strongly believe in morally, relationally, and/or spiritually.

It is time to remove the "silencer" of fear, intimidation and anxiety. Some of you may find it extremely difficult to have the confidence to speak because of intimidation that has tried to control you. Some of you have even had word curses spoken over you. Once you identify the false power of intimidation and the powerlessness of curses, you will take authority over them. A whole new world is there for you to discover when you reach that point.

There are other things as well that can keep a person in this silent world of fear. Trauma from a surgery or accident, actions of abuse or neglect, near-death experiences, rejection/abandonment, mind control – all these and more can settle over your heart. Sometimes these experiences can leave one feeling as though she has two or more identities. Learn to lay your hand on your heart and rebuke it. Tell it to leave in Jesus' name.

You have a voice given to you by God. It is time to take action and to cross over into victory by recognizing this fact. It may take role-playing with another person to speak out what you feel or take hold of a microphone to learn to use one or record yourself on your laptop. Just get used to hearing your own voice. As you gain confidence and speak out truths from God's Word in prayer or make decrees or declarations for your own family, you will grow by leaps and bounds in authority and confidence. It is God in you that wants to speak out. He has given you a very special voice and there are certain people who truly need to hear what you have to say.

Some people are loud and boisterous; others are very quiet-spoken. Which are you? How would you classify your voice? Do you like to sing? I was told I could not carry a tune in a bucket, but now I sing and sing and sing. God has loosed my vocal chords to sing alto. What a miracle that is to me. I longed to sing to God and to minister to Him. He has given me the desire of my heart. He will do the same for you. People have told me that I have a radio voice and to get on the radio. So I did broadcast on the Hour of Power Radio Program for a few years. People recognized my voice wherever I went. It was fun to do.

Let's get serious. You have a voice, right? Just as Job did, use your voice to say, "Lord, awaken my heart to the anointing in me for the new season." Stand up and prophecy for His light to shine each day into your family, your house, your city. Just do it.

Use your voice to proclaim, **"There is no God like the God I serve. He lifts me up and out of the dark places."** Decree your identity in Christ. Patricia King has learned this truth and published DECREE. A precious gem of a booklet she testifies in praying and speaking the words daily for 2 hours to prepare her heart and mind for the day. Sing the Psalms. Do battle with any signs of resistance, stubbornness, and wrong attitudes toward God and command it to go. Release the sound of your voice. Release prayer and stand with the voice of the Lord, decreeing His promises and blessings. A great tool for this is Sylvia Gunter's book on the You are Blessed in the Names of God.

It is so important and so amazing that we are God's voice on earth. We are a triumphant reserve in the army of God – let revelation come to us, Lord. God does give us revelation, even when we are in the hard places. We must hear from Him. Repent of leaning on others to get through the battle. Wait for His Word. Absolutely, a door will open when you need it. You step through and watch God move.

In the tenth chapter of the book of John we hear Jesus say that His sheep hear His voice. If we are born again we are His sheep and we do hear His voice. And when we are obedient and quick to respond to His voice, our voice – His words coming forth from us – become very important in the earth. There is much fire coming out when we pray. The enemy is fearful of true prayer. It must be our desire to do what the Father is doing, to say what the Father is saying. He gave us a voice to use.

Read Psalm 23 and 24. Learn to listen to His voice. Know that when you are walking through the valley of the shadow of death, He will lead and guide you. You can say, "God, here I am. Use me."

Now is the time to interpret dreams. Don't be afraid. This is a season for knowing your dreams. Joseph was a dreamer and interpreted dreams. Claim your vision. Write it down and pray over it. You will literally birth your dream into being through prayer.

God has given you a voice. Take dominion in Him. He is calling us to do just that. Release your God-given Kingdom authority. We are to occupy the earth. Let heaven invade your space! God wants us to occupy until He comes again. Possess your territory – your sphere of influence. Engage and bring change. Manifest God's dominion in the midst of Satan's presence.

At the Biblical birth of humanity, Adam and Eve were given dominion. Much of the church has forgotten how to take dominion, how to take back what is theirs. A picture of the church getting weaker, huddled inside with no power is not a Biblical picture. The New Testament church is not frail, dying, or struggling. Read the book of Ephesians, particularly chapter 5. This is a time of restoration and inheritance, but there is still a battle in which we are engaged. There is always a battle when moving forward following the Lord. Satan hates for the saint to know their authority, and regain ground stolen by his lies. Jesus the

Bridegroom is returning to receive His glorious Bride, not one who defeated and powerless.

Jesus said that His kingdom is not of this world nor is it political. Rather, His kingdom is spiritually discerned. He said that His bride will be of no form for she is spirit and truth refined by fire as pure transparent gold. We can know she is near because of her purity – the sound of heaven released on earth. We will hear the sound of roaring thunder coming from heaven, mighty waters flowing, warring dance on her feet to crush principalities, and armored light to stand and shine forever in the presence of her King.

We have seen a decline of integrity, righteousness and justice as a country. These areas are:

Lance Wallnau's 7 mountains are:

1. **Government**
2. **Business**
3. **Media**
4. **Arts and Entertainment**
5. **Education**
6. **Family**
7. **Religion**

When we occupy and show His character and nature in these areas, He blesses the work of our hands. When we don't occupy and show His character and nature, poverty and lack in each area occurs.

How do we take back what the enemy has stolen from us? We use our voice, our keys, our love, our strategies, and God's word. We occupy with dominion. It is high time to cross over into the new day, new season, and new spiritual shift of our destiny by letting go of the old and by joining God in what He is doing. Sow into the Kingdom plan of God. Be strong, be courageous.

Jesus exercised ultimate dominion everywhere He went. He changed the atmosphere and the hearts of the people by His holiness, truth, justice, and righteousness. He has given us the right to manifest dominion and shout, "I will not relinquish my watch." We must speak the Word of God into the atmosphere, being salt and light on the earth.

You have authority to exercise dominion wherever God sends you. Wherever your feet touch the ground, declare peace and the good news of the gospel. You have authority to decree, "Get out of my city, Satan. Get out of my home, my marriage, and my relationships." Speak it and declare it until you see it manifested. You can take your stand against drug and sex traffickers and the like. Decree that they are being exposed to public eye, caught and prosecuted to the full measure of justice. Declare into the very atmosphere, "This atmosphere is no longer conducive to Satan's darkness. I have the right from God by faith to see things change. I will not bow to 'cultural conversion' and loss of identity and purpose" Take your stand. Release the sound of Heaven. Release His fragrance, His grace, His love. Now is the hour. Now is the time.

Women and youth are arising for the harvest. They are armed and ready for battle to take back what the enemy has stolen. Giant-killers and dragon-slayers are arising as His hidden ones who have great integrity for His perfect timing for victory. A move of God is on the horizon and coming to your city, youth and the world.

God is exposing error in the church and major deception that has been in place by the enemy for centuries. Use your voice – refuse to let intimidation and fear silence you or allow mockers to stand in your way. Be fearless and ROAR. Laugh at the enemy.

An example of what I am writing about occurred on a trip in 2013 to Wales to minister. Upon the team's arrival on the land, a lighthouse glass ceiling in North Wales shattered, as a sign and wonder to those practicing divination that God sees them in their darkness. I believe it was a manifestation of God's coming judgment on the darkness of occult practices in Devron. He has said, "Enough! I have had enough. No more witchcraft or idolatry or sexual immorality." God must act in defense of His holy name.

Lord, right now in the name of Jesus I break the stronghold of fear and intimidation off the reader. I ask for boldness and courage and great faith to be granted in their hearts to endure till the end and to do whatever You would have them to do.

These two spiritual voices are God's and the devils. Be aware of these main differences between the two. It will help you determine whose voice to listen to and who's to shun.

God's Voice

- Stills you
- Leads you
- Reassures you
- Enlightens you
- Encourages you
- Comforts you
- Calms you
- Convicts you

Satan's Voice

- Rushes you
- Pushes you
- Frightens you
- Confuses you
- Discourages you
- Worries you
- Obsesses you
- Condemns you

Since communication is the key to life and praying for change in perspective is so important, it is imperative that we continue to speak Godly things over our lives and those of others. The following is a list of positive Biblical confessions to say over yourself and your family.

1. **I am the righteousness of God in Jesus Christ.**
2. **I walk in divine health because the Word of God says that by the stripes of Jesus Christ I am healed. My family and I are healed—physically, mentally, emotionally, and spiritually.**
3. **I have wisdom and revelation knowledge.**
4. **I am blessed and I am a blessing everywhere I go and in everything I do.**
5. **I have favor with all people and with God.**
6. **We are ministers of the Gospel of Christ Jesus.**
7. **I can do all things through Christ who strengthens me. I am strong and I do exploits—bold deeds and daring acts—for my God.**
8. **I am patient, kind, holy, and pure.**
9. **I love all people for my God shows no partiality.**
10. **I have prosperity in all areas of life—spiritually, financially, physically, mentally, emotionally, and socially.**
11. **My children are saved, Spirit-filled, and married to born-again, full-gospel mates who walk in the wise counsel of God.**
12. **My entire household is blessed in our deeds. We are blessed when we come in and when we go out.**
13. **I know God's voice and I always obey what He tells me.**
14. **We take good care of our bodies. We eat right, look good, and feel well.**
15. **The love of God has been shed abroad in my heart by the Holy Spirit.**
16. **I do all of my work with excellence and great prudence.**
17. **I am creative because the Holy Spirit lives in me.**

18. **I love to praise and worship God.**
19. **I am purposed that my mouth shall not transgress.**
20. **I will speak forth the righteousness of God.**
21. **I have humbled myself and God has exalted me.**
22. **I am a giver. It is more blessed to give than to receive. I love to give.**
23. **I cast all of my cares on the Lord and He cares for me.**
24. **I don't give the devil a foothold in my life. I resist the devil and he has to flee from me.**
25. **I do not have a spirit of fear, but of power, love, and a sound mind.**
26. **I do not fear man.**
27. **I am a new creature in Christ. Old things have passed away. Behold, all things have become new in me.**
28. **I have died and have been raised with Christ. I am now seated in heavenly places in Christ Jesus. I am dead to sin and alive unto righteousness.**
29. **I am a doer of the Word.**
30. **I meditate on the Word all the day long.**
31. **I am not passive about anything, but I deal with things immediately.**
32. **I do not judge my brethren in Christ after the flesh for I am a spiritual man and I myself am judge by no one.**
33. **I take every thought captive to the obedience of Jesus the Christ.**
34. **I cast down imaginations and every high and lofty thought that exalts itself against the knowledge of God.**
35. **I am a responsible person.**
36. **I enjoy and rise to every responsibility in Jesus.**
37. **I have been set free of addictions of any kind.**

So remember – you have a voice, a very special voice like no one else's. It is for a purpose. It is to be used to declare; decree; pray; sing;

speak out truth, justice, righteousness, and holiness. Let your voice be a human shofar. It's time to get in the game. Let your voice resonate with heaven's truths. Release the gems of your testimony to bring glory to God. Just do it. You will be glad you did.

CHAPTER 4:

The Power of the Right Choice

Choosing to change – what is the definition of choice? Choice means act of your will; to choose between right and wrong; to discern lie from truth. A decision is arrived at by logical deduction. An example: Do I want to be a victim or a survivor? Do I want fear to control my thoughts and make me a negative person, or do I want to choose to be a faith-filled positive person who is thankful for God's love?

In Isaiah 56:4-5 we read the following:

> "[4] *For thus said the Lord unto the eunuchs that keep my Sabbaths, and choose the things that please me, and take hold of my covenant;*
>
> [5] *even unto them will I give in mine house and within my walls a place and a name better than of sons and*

of daughters: I will give them an everlasting name, that shall not be cut off."

We have the power and ability to make better choices for our lives. Emotional decisions based on feelings lead to disastrous consequences. A belief system based on truth and wisdom is best. What is coming out of our mouth is what we really believe.

God gives us the free will and power to choose. He has empowered us to make choices for ourselves. No matter what is going on in our lives, we do always have the power to choose between following the Word of the Lord or some other voice. Lining up our lives to be Christ-like does require the denial of self and the renewing of the mind through the Word of God.

There are many elements that affect the decision-making process. It is so valuable to take a look at your decision and take the time to ask the Lord, "What do You want in my life today?" Spending time listening to His voice helps to discern a spiritual decision from a fleshly one. Look to Him to guide you.

Humility is part of wise decision making. Pride and arrogance greatly interfere with the process. The flesh wants to be right, wants to dominate. It takes perseverance and determination to remain steady in our witness for God. Thankfulness plays a huge part as well. Even forgiveness, or the lack thereof, has a role in what we decide to do, think, say, and believe.

Other elements that can greatly impact our decision-making on matters of the flesh, of the soul are a strong desire to be right, no matter what, will sway the outcome, rage, anger, jealousy and bitterness. Falling to the influence of emotions has a terrible effect. Looking at circumstances rather than His Word does not bring the desired results. Listening to any voice other than that of the Lord will take your decision in the wrong direction.

But there are also elements that dynamically impact our ability to make great choices for the Lord. Hebrews 7:25 tells us that Jesus ever lives to make intercession for us. He wants to help you make the right decisions. Ask Him to be part of the process. He empowers you through His Spirit. Train yourself to speak by faith His powerful words of change. God will work it out. Praise the Lord at all times. Learn to stay in an attitude of praise.

Ruth Story of Choice

In learning to make Godly decisions, He has given us a tremendous example in the story of Ruth. If you will take the time to read the short book of Ruth in the Old Testament you will be rewarded richly.

Ruth was a Moabite who became a follower of the one true God. Her life testifies to her faith and her loyalty. The story revolves around the death of Ruth's first husband and her decisions that followed that life-changing event. Widowed Ruth could have chosen to go back to her own people, the Moabites. But she instead chose to walk with Naomi, her mother-in-law and follow after the God of Abraham.

By making the Godly choice she became a woman of glory. She obeyed the wise instruction she received from Naomi to prepare herself to meet Boaz, her kinsman redeemer. I believe she was healed emotionally from the loss and grief of losing her husband, perhaps even from the generational curse of her own people, the Moabite. God prepared her as she humbled herself at the feet of her kinsman redeemer. She was cleansed, renewed, restored and made ready for the next step.

Ruth pursued and positioned herself for promotion as one of the redeemed. She was chosen to be in the lineage of Jesus, becoming an ancestress of David the King. Ruth drew near to her destiny to receive the blessings of covenant. She was watchful and was careful not to miss her divine appointment. She believed and was counted among the righteous. She leaned in and loved forward to experience Godly union. She changed her destiny by choosing opportunity. She was cloaked in glory because she was destined to carry His glory and walk with His people. Fear did not apprehend her. Her past did not detain her. Her future drew her God-ward. Nothing could change her mind because she chose to change and be one with God.

Ruth could have identified herself as a victim of her circumstances and made her way back into idolatry. She could have believed the lie that she was not good enough to be used by God or even be redeemed. But instead she believed in victory and the hopeful accepting words of her mother-in-law who was a wise woman who loved God. Ruth chose well and changed the world's destiny.

Reality Exercise

A huge decision you will make probably more than once in your life is this: Will I be a victim or a victor? To help you be certain to choose victory, the following exercise is a beneficial aid.

1. **Sit comfortably and inhale, saying, "Abba, I belong to Jesus. Exhale, saying, "You are my reality." Do this several times, relaxing as you do so.**
2. **Declare your desire for wholeness, according to John 5:5-6. Do you want to be made whole? Tell the Lord this is your desire.**

   I. **What, if anything, makes it difficult to say yes?**

      a. **We want someone else to do it for us, but healing comes from one-on-one encounters with God (John 5:7)**

      b. **We must agree that the new is better, even though the old is familiar and comfortable. (Luke 5:36, 39)**

      c. **We must recognize the tendency to remain paralyzed in denial. Denial is not okay. (Joshua 10:12-15)**

   II. **Resist the temptation to stay stuck in the sameness and declare, "I will participate in the victory that is mine in Christ Jesus." Press through.**

3. **Ask the Lord to tell you what He wants you to do in order to walk in victory in your specific situation. Open your**

mind and heart to receive His direction. Expect Him to reveal His truth to you.

4. **Thank the Lord for His answers and for His love and care for you. Reaffirm with your voice, "I am victorious in Christ Jesus. I am not a victim. I have been set free."**

For some the process will become a much deeper journey with the need to destroy chains of abuse and storms of negative counter-productive emotions. It will be imperative to deal effectively with issues of grief, innocence lost, and childhood stolen. Bitterness must be done away with through the process of forgiveness. Guilt is yet another level that must be done away with entirely. There is no wholeness without this step. The voice must proclaim these freedoms and claim healing at these deep levels. Often this process requires the help of a trained pastoral counselor. If you become overwhelmed in trying to walk out any issues within, please do not remain alone. Seek help from a loving and well-equipped Christian counselor. Pray and ask the Lord to direct you in this. Through this person, God will love you into wholeness.

For some the path of Godly decision making will bring up all kinds of deep internal pains and hurts. Know that Jesus has already provided healing for each and every one of these. There is great hope for you and endless love in Him. This path calls for the courage to be honest with yourself and God and with those working to help you. Hold fast to Godly relationships in your life for support and love as you move through the process. The end result will be victorious and life-changing even as Ruth's decisions changed her life and destiny.

Healing of the Lost Child

Lord, let me see a lost child; let me be a part of the whole.

A waif, a small child with her head hung low

Frail and insignificant to the outside world

No love did she know or receive.

She came into vision by the Lord's hand

To be brought back to the woman she now is

She beckoned to belong, to be a part of the whole.

She called out of the darkness of her betrayal and shame

To say, "Love me, bless me, nurture me, hug me, and believe me."

She asked, "Can I trust you?" Lie: You are not of any value.

"Yes," Jesus said, "Come, come sit on My lap awhile.

Let me bless you, shower love upon you, rock you,

And yes, I believe you, for you see, I was there.

And, I will never leave you nor forsake you.

Come, be a part of the whole."

It is simply a lie that says that God is a punisher, that He has judged and rejected you, that you must perform just right in order to be accepted by Him. No, God is the God of love and grace. Read Hebrews 12:18-24 here to see that we are now called to a great place of joy. We are free to be ourselves in Him.

> *"[18] For ye are not come unto the mount that might be touched, and that burned with fire, nor unto blackness, and darkness, and tempest, [19] and the sound of a trumpet, and the voice of words; which voice they that heard entreated that the word should not be spoken to them any more: [20] (for they could not endure that which was commanded, And if so much as a beast touch the mountain, it shall be stoned, or thrust through with a dart: [21] and so terrible was the sight, that Moses said, I exceedingly fear and quake:) [22] but ye are come unto mount Sion, and unto the city of the living God, the*

heavenly Jerusalem, and to an innumerable company of angels, [23] to the general assembly and church of the firstborn, which are written in heaven, and to God the Judge of all, and to the spirits of just men made perfect, [24] and to Jesus the mediator of the new covenant, and to the blood of sprinkling, that speak better things than that of Abel."

Once you have received Jesus and realize that you are accepted in the eyes of God, relax. Enjoy His everlasting boundless love. Praise Him! You have an assurance of His grace, of His empowerment in your life. You can become aware of His moment-to-moment presence with you, of His intimacy with you, His nearness, His kind listening and responses to you. He fulfills all in all and supplies all your needs. His Spirit indwells you and equips you, enables you in your weakness to do all things. Through faith is how we experience all of Him.

God has always intended for us to live by His wisdom, by His ways. He has always planned for us to abide richly in Him, in intimacy with Him. He came to set the captive free; no mountain, no tribulation can stop us in Him! This relationship produces good fruit in us; abiding in the vine is the key.

One of the greatest mysteries to our walk with God is the fact that there is nothing we can do to make Him love us, to make Him accept us. He loves and accepts us through the finished work of Jesus – nothing more, nothing less. It is His work, not ours. It is a wonderful exciting journey of grace as He holds our hand. Because of what Jesus did for us, there is no room for condemnation to dwell in our heart and mind. We are truly free in Him. In this abundance of life is fullness of joy and we need to experience and express that joy. That is a tremendous part of our testimony that Jesus has made a difference in us.

Poem

I was regretting the past and fearing the future.

Suddenly my Lord was speaking:

"My name is I AM." He paused. I waited. He continued.

"When you live in the past, with its mistakes and regrets,

It is hard. I am not there.

My name is not 'I was'.

When you live in the future, with its problems and fears,

It is hard. I am not there.

My name is not 'I WILL BE'.

When you live in this moment, it is not hard; I am here."

Did you notice that when Ruth had made her decision to follow Naomi and move forward in a direction toward God, the Bible does not tell us that she sat and moped and cried and spoke negatively about her strange new path or about the circumstances that brought her there? She kept her peace and moved forward in faith.

In the same way that Ruth walked in faith and stayed positive, trusting in God to see her through and make a way for her, so we must do the same in our life circumstances. Therefore, make it a point to keep a positive confession with your voice, ever resting in the promises of God. When asked about the circumstances of your life, it is good to respond with, "It is well with my soul." As you continue to walk in this way, just like Ruth, you will see the barriers in your life come down in every area – health, finances, and relationships.

The world does enjoy a negative report! How it tries to get us to align with the enemy and not with God. King David struggled with it when he lusted for Bathsheba. Samson lost his sight by revealing the secret of his strength. We are no different than they. We are to exercise Godly discipline over ourselves – over our flesh – and stay focused on Him. Our goal is to produce fruit for God.

The Bible gives us power to become the sons of God when we believe. The Holy Spirit comes and empowers us. We are to look for the power of God, not lean on ourselves. We live in a "self-help" time. Your local bookstore is filled to overflowing with books on every type of "fix yourself" topic imaginable. All of them fail completely. All of them fall far short of the power of God. It is that God-ordained power that we are so desperately seeking. It alone will satisfy. God's power gives you strength to rise above the flesh.

Through the Lord Jesus we do have control over our thoughts and attitudes. Though the flesh might scream and cry and pitch a fit, we do have the ability in Him to rise above the fray within and exercise control over our fleshly desires. At the point of decision the flesh can be very strong and very noisy. That is why it is so important to have spent quality time in the Word of God to know His ways, His thoughts, and His desires – His will for your life. From His Word you draw the courage to make the stand to follow the Spirit not the flesh and move on toward God. We are told by Paul to let go of the past and press on to the high calling in Christ Jesus. We accomplish this one decision at a time.

Take a few moments to think about it. What areas are out of control in your life just now? Be bold and courageous to take this up with God in prayer and find His wise counsel and direction for your life. Trust Him to bring your life into Godly balance.

CHAPTER 5:

Overcomer — God of the Breakthrough

The nature of God is as important as the Word of God. The Body of Christ is going through a new season, and as a part of that, you are in your own season. Some things do not seem right by alignment, but God promotes and brings change.

Today women are breaking into a new place of authority, a new season. They are breaking through the walls of resistance of flesh and demonic strongholds. They are breaking into their destiny to preach, to teach, and to prophecy. They are breaking out of the lies that have been used against them for 2000 years or more. He is Lord Perizim – the Lord of the breakthrough. Malachi 3:6 tells us that God never changes.

God desires for each person to break out of bondage and fulfill His divine purpose for her life. And in that process, no one skips a season; they come to everyone. Trying to catapult one's self past the uncomfortable parts of the journey does not work. God says that He will do this in our life in due season. Being in the right place at the right time is a spiritual thing.

It is helpful to recognize from the very beginning that our biggest weakness will be magnified by the enemy if we do not stand our ground and take our place. Some have been so reluctant and are so wounded by spiritual abuse from the church that they are held back by the trauma of it all. It is as if they are asleep and might miss the hour of God's timing. God truly brings to each a door of opportunity to serve and to go to war for what is rightfully theirs by the Holy Spirit. Today is a "now" time; it is high time for women and men.

A look into the life of David reveals a time when he himself held back (for his own set of reasons that seemed reasonable to him at the time), and lusted for Bathsheba. He thus gave into his fleshly desires and wants, a decision that was met with the most serious of consequences.

Being of two minds, or double-minded, never receives anything from God. In fact, God cannot really use us if we are double-minded. That's why it is so very important to make clear decisions, especially choosing to be aligned with God in His ways, His calendar, His redemptive plan. It is His plan that none would perish, but all would have everlasting life. We must become a part of that plan.

Joan of Arc once said, "One life is all we have and we live it as we believe in living it. But to sacrifice what you are and to live without belief, that is a fate more terrible than dying." Her courage in the face of challenges to see revival pour out in her nation is inspiring. We need courage and boldness that cannot be quenched as well. Women in ministry will be marked by a courage that cannot be quenched. They will truly live.

By definition, a breakthrough is a revolution, advancement, innovation, improvement, important discovery that has far-reaching and dramatic effect, removal of a barrier to progress, penetration of enemy lines, and bringing public attention to an issue. God's women today are experiencing breakthrough in so many areas of life.

The most dynamic breakthrough Godly women and men are experiencing in this time is in the area of Kingdom authority. The positions of men and women are being righted, allowing women to walk in their Godly authority and flow in the gifts of the Holy Spirit.

Why is this taking place so dynamically today, now? I believe it is the hour of the greatest harvest of souls for God the earth has ever seen. Very simply, God has need of us. This transformation is taking place within the Body of Christ around the globe. Godly women are being granted an open door of favor to the nations as well as to their neighborhoods. Locally and abroad God is working mightily through us.

In my travels and ministering in various parts of the United States and the world I continue to see God calling and working through His precious servants. Some of these have been hidden for a long time, but have been and are being prepared – equipped and trained – to dive into the deep water of His River of revival and reformation. Women and youth are being connected supernaturally to see healings, miracles, signs, and wonders by the preaching and teaching of the Word of God. It is a mighty display of the power of the Gospel of Jesus.

The Kingdom of the Gospel is ruled by kings and priests. David was a king and a priest. His intimacy with God helped him prevail for God brought vindication against his enemy. This gave David a firm foundation upon which to stand and rule.

Jesus made it clear that church is where two or three are gathered. Two people can make up the fullness of the church and it multiplies. Church develops from there in local settings with common shared vision. We do not need a new denomination. We need to let the people go and be all they are called to be.

The Holy Spirit will lead and guide us into all truth. We must learn to trust the Holy Spirit. We have to seek the Spirit and God's Word and begin to learn what God wants for us and of us. This is how we mature in the Lord; we make mistakes, but we learn systematically every day. We will eventually carry our own weight. As this takes place both individually and as a church, strong community develops.

In Genesis 12:1-3 we find the following account regarding Abram (later to be called Abraham):

> *"[1] Now the Lord had said unto Abram, Get thee out of thy country, and from thy kindred, and from thy father's house, unto a land that I will shew thee: [2] and I*

will make of thee a great nation, and I will bless thee, and make thy name great; and thou shalt be a blessing: [3] and I will bless them that bless thee, and curse him that curses thee: and in thee shall all families of the earth be blessed."

The "call of Abraham" means to break out in order to receive the blessings raining down from God in Heaven. Abram received really just two action words from God: 1) get up, and 2) go where I send you.

In Hebrews 9:8-15 we read:

"Holy Ghost this signifying, that the way into the holiest of all was not yet made manifest, while as the first tabernacle was yet standing: [9] which was a figure for the time then present, in which were offered both gifts and sacrifices, that could not make him that did the service perfect, as pertaining to the conscience; [10] which stood only in meats and drinks, and divers washings, and carnal ordinances, imposed on them until the time of reformation.

[11] But Christ being come an high priest of good things to come, by a greater and more perfect tabernacle, not made with hands, that is to say, not of this building; [12] neither by the blood of goats and calves, but by his own blood he entered in once into the holy place, having obtained eternal redemption for us. [13] For if the blood of bulls and of goats, and the ashes of a heifer sprinkling the unclean, sanctified to the purifying of the flesh: [14] how much more shall the blood of Christ, who through the eternal Spirit offered himself without spot to God, purge your conscience from dead works to serve the living God?

> 15 *And for this cause he is the mediator of the New Testament that by means of death, for the redemption of the transgressions that were under the first testament, they which are called might receive the promise of eternal inheritance."*

It is time for a revolution, time for us to break out of our carnal and worldly life paths and enter into all that God has provided for us in Jesus. First of all, we have to get up and go – break out! This is what Abram did and he became the father of the faithful. He walked in faith and obedience to what God told him. Believing and trusting God is the bottom line of immediate obedience. If you truly believe God you are prepared to respond to do whatever God tells you to do. How do we become faithful? Faithfulness is established when we operate in the faith of doing and obeying the works of the Lord.

Abraham was a gentile. He was Babylonian by birth and Assyrian by nationality. He crossed over the Euphrates River and became the first Hebrew. The Hebrew word ebar means he crossed over to the other side. Abraham, one day you were over here and now you are over there.

Spiritually speaking, God has translated us from the kingdom of darkness into the Kingdom of His dear Son. This is eternal life now. If you are born again you were in death; now you are in life. You crossed over. There is no grave to hold you down. Eternal life is what you are living now.

Even Abraham, the father of the faithful, got hung up in Haran, a place that was not his destination. Things became confused and comfortable and Abraham had to come back into God's plan and move on. We, too, can easily become comfortable and like our own beliefs, even those that are contrary to what God tells us. If we are not mindful to stay obedient and connected to Him, God can move on and we are left wondering what happened.

It is pretty much human nature for us to want to settle and be secure; we do not like to be uncomfortable or do what we consider hard things. It is also part of the carnal nature to be greatly influenced by the pressures that come from others. Peer pressure presents itself at all ages; it is not just a problem for teens or children. We encounter it in our church and community. The pressure is on to conform to the norm. God, as a gentleman, will never force us to make a move. We may choose to remain in our situation if that's what you want, but we will miss out on so much that God has for us by staying there when He's told us to move on forward.

Very few are pioneers who want to break the mold to step out beyond the known and the comfortable. The pioneer will do the hard thing. They will not conform to the world's standard, no matter the cost. So many people are willing to go with the flow, not wanting to take on the challenge of change. One has but to study history to see that it is a never ending array of crystallization. God cannot do anything with the people who are boxed in, who will not move out and obey. The one boxed in doesn't even usually realize where they are. There is blindness and a deception that goes hand in hand with it.

Can a person break out of that box? Yes! But the only way to do so is to repent and return to God. The Hebrew word teshuva means to return to the right way of God.

God told Noah that it was going to rain...a lot! It had never rained. What? Most people did not listen to him. Some of what God speaks to us is logical; many times it is not. Many times what He says to our hearts will disagree strongly with what we see, hear, feel, and think. Just as it must have seemed illogical to his neighbors for Noah to be building that ark, it may seem illogical to us to do what God is telling us to do.

Obedience on our part will probably not look like the norm around us. How wonderful it is, though, to follow in obedience and to see it suddenly work! Then we understand and embrace more fully what God is doing through us.

Abraham left his family and all the comforts of home. He was a stranger, Ker, and a pilgrim in his own land. It probably looked strange to those around him to watch him pack up and leave like that.

Moses had the same kinds of experiences. The night that God was delivering the children of Israel from the bondage of Egypt, he was told what would have seemed strange to others. The children of Israel were told to put blood on the door-posts of their houses. Think about it. To those who didn't know its meaning, it would have seemed like a nasty distasteful thing to do. It is not in decorating books or home improvement magazines! But God was doing a specific new thing and their obedience was absolutely critical to the outcome He desired for them.

God was going to make it possible for them to break out of Egyptian bondage by ultimately going through the midst of the Red Sea. God's strategy is super-logical. His plan liberated the Israelites and killed their enemies in one move. They were delivered in one great swoop.

When God says to move on, why are we standing still and not moving? We may start walking toward the brick wall with nothing apparently happening. Then suddenly the doors open and we walk through! That is faith to walk at God's response.

David never used the same strategy from one battle to the next. He always sought the Lord and the Lord revealed to him the plan of victory. When fighting against the Philistines David was told by God to listen and hear the noise in the mulberry trees. You can read about it in Second Samuel, chapter five. If David had used yesterday's battle strategy he would have lost. He fought the same enemy in the same place, but God gave him different strategies. He followed exactly what God told him to do. David relied on the Lord and the Lord always led him well.

How very important it is today to not become a stale Christian. We, too, must learn to ever rely on the Lord for leadership and guidance. Ask for fresh understanding and insight for each day's situation. We cannot depend on rancid oil. That's how we end up with "stinking thinking" and "hardening of the attitudes". We must have fresh oil – fresh anointing – every day. It is a day-by-day strategy. We must seek Him daily and follow Jesus, one step at a time.

Look at Ephesians 2:11-18:

> *"[11] Wherefore remember, that ye being in time past Gentiles in the flesh, who are called Uncircumcision by that which is called the Circumcision in the flesh made by hands; [12] that at that time ye were without Christ, being*

aliens from the commonwealth of Israel, and strangers from the covenants of promise, having no hope, and without God in the world: [13] but now in Christ Jesus ye who sometimes were far off are made nigh by the blood of Christ. [14] For he is our peace, who hath made both one, and hath broken down the middle wall of partition between us; [15] having abolished in his flesh the enmity, even the law of commandments contained in ordinances; for to make in himself of twain one new man, so making peace; [16] and that he might reconcile both unto God in one body by the cross, having slain the enmity thereby: [17] and came and preached peace to you which were afar off, and to them that were nigh. [18] for through him we both have access by one Spirit unto the Father."

The old covenant was exclusive to Israel. But then Jesus came and died and rose again. By His death, burial, and resurrection the new covenant is now openly offered to everyone on the planet. The wall of partition has been removed! Jesus brought the gospel, the good news, to everyone. Breakthrough came! Now we are to go to the whole world.

Read on through the third chapter of Ephesians to see that Paul goes on to further explain the mystery of the Kingdom gospel which is to bring gentiles to the gospel by the shed blood of Jesus Christ. This was revealed by the Holy Spirit. The apostles were inspired by the Holy Spirit. There will always be mysteries in life. There is always a key to each one, even in our everyday lives.

God uses things in a person's everyday life to do His bidding. What do you have in your hand today? God asked Moses what he had in his hand. It was a stick – it became the rod of God. Elijah told the woman in Second Kings chapter 4 to go borrow as many vessels as she could find. She filled all the vessels with oil. When the vessels ran out, the supernatural supply of oil stopped. She sold it all and paid her debt plus had money on which to live. God will do in proportion to what we expect Him to do.

We can allow ourselves to stay in the box or we can choose to follow God and exit our comfortable box. We can choose to engage in the process of leaving. It is a grand adventure with God.

It never ceases to amaze me how much we can love the status-quo, the mess around us. It can even be painful, but still we have a tendency to want to stay put. We find so many ways to cope with the misery or disappointment or pain of it and just remain locked away in our self-imposed prisons.

Break out! Throw the doors wide open and flow with God. We can operate in an arena of organized chaos. His purpose is in it all. If we will keep our focus and hold steady in our obedience to Him, our circumstances will change and He brings us around. He is orchestrating all the pieces of the puzzle. Follow Him one step at a time. Walk with God; move forward.

We must also walk in love toward each other, making space for one another. Don't force anyone into anything. God doesn't do that to us, nor does He want us to treat others in that way. We need people to be free to function in the gifts and talents God has placed within them. We must all contribute from those gifts within and experience His joy from doing it. We must allow space for this to happen.

True community is all about learning to flow, all participating as one. Get away from performance-based Christianity. I believe God is leading us into a place of oneness together. Growing up and maturing will become visible and discernible upon us all as we continue in our love walk in Him.

In this environment of Godly love and acceptance the age variances will fall away as well. Invite the young people, the teens and children to take part in sharing scripture and Bible truths with the congregation. Great skills are honed in this way. Everyone is accepted; everyone has something to say.

Historically, especially in the Middle Ages, Christianity kept people superstitious, ignorant of truth, dependent on controlling priests. If the people didn't obey the leaders explicitly they were told they would have no salvation. Can you see the risk involved in letting the sheep out who need to be fed the truth?

We are told to preach the gospel of the Kingdom. We as Christians are not meant to get saved over and over again. There is a need for maturity in the instructions of God and in our walk with Him. Ephesians 4:11-13 talks of God's plan for equipping the saints. We should be preparing all the sheep to go and do the works of the ministry. This is very clear.

> *"[11] And he gave some, apostles; and some, prophets; and some, evangelists; and some, pastors and teachers; [12] for the perfecting of the saints, for the work of the ministry, for the edifying of the body of Christ: [13] till we all come in the unity of the faith, and of the knowledge of the Son of God, unto a perfect man, unto the measure of the stature of the fullness of Christ:"*

Right now in your situation, it is time to have a break-out session so that God can use you! The Lord sees and provides for our every need. You do have the opportunity to hear from the Lord now. He tells us in His word that He sees and hears us. Make your decision to be obedient to His voice in your life. Father, we thank you for your provision. Give us the grace to walk in faith.

You will find it helpful to meditate on the following scriptures in order to help build up your faith and strength in Him. We are told to fear not.

- **Isaiah 41:10**
- **Isaiah 41:13**
- **Isaiah 54:4Deuteronomy 31:6**
- **Ephesians 3:20**
- **Joshua 1**

I am grateful for the many deep teachings and insights from Dr. John D. Garr, Ph. D., of the Hebraic Christian Global Community.

CHAPTER 6:

Fear, Shame, and Control — Enough!

The ability of fear to control my mind and emotions for most of my life was very significant. By the Spirit I saw fear as an anvil of strong iron from the top of my head to the base of my skull and it covered my face. It was a fortress filled with lies that I had to unlearn. I had to renew my mind with God's word by journaling and discovering scriptural context for what I was trying to overcome. 1 John 4:18 says "perfect love drives out fear..."

A cloak of shame covered my face. I could never see or accept that God had created me pretty or attractive. This was because of the rejection as a middle child and divorced home in 1950's, poverty because we had very little income, and wrong decision-making in my life. Due to fear and anxiety as a young child, I was plagued with infirmity. Near-death hospital experiences haunted my mind and life from 14 years of age to 56.

At age 38 in my journey to freedom I was so anxiety-bound that I was in bed for three days and could not remember how to open the front door or call my mother. I couldn't even remember how to use the phone. I collapsed in an emotional heap on the floor drooling and unconscious. The power of the fear of abandonment was a trigger in me from when my father left me at four years old. From that point on, when someone would leave me alone, I would comfort myself with food.

God delivered me from all of the above and so much more. I stand as a testimony and a witness of the power of the cross and His complete obedience to love me to freedom in Christ. Trust me – He will cut the roots of the curses, set us free by the resurrection power and give you Jesus hugs in the process of becoming whole. His blood is sufficient to break any demonic strongholds. His Word is alive and sharp to separate truth from lies. Are you ready to take the challenge of renewing your mind and being transformed by His great grace and love?

Fear and Love

Love will be the distinguishing characteristic of the Bride of Christ. Luke 6:27-36 tells us to:

> *"11 And he gave some, apostles; and some, prophets; and some, evangelists; and some, pastors and teachers; 12 for the perfecting of the saints, for the work of the ministry, for the edifying of the body of Christ: 13 till we all come in the unity of the faith, and of the knowledge of the Son of God, unto a perfect man, unto the measure of the stature of the fullness of Christ:*
>
> *32 But if you love those who love you, what credit is that to you? For even sinners love those who love them. 33 And if you do good to those who do good to you, what credit is that to you? For even sinners do the same. 34 And if you lend to those from whom you hope to receive back, what credit is that to you? For even sinners lend to sinners to receive as much back. 35 But love your enemies, do well, and lend, hoping for nothing in*

return; and your reward will be great, and you will be sons of the Most High. For He is kind to the unthankful and evil. [36] Therefore be merciful, just as your Father also is merciful."

John 13:35 goes on to say,

"By this shall all men know that ye are my disciples, if ye have love one to another."

Fear is the greatest stronghold in the Body of Christ. The Messiah's bride is not to be fearful, but full of love for her coming Bridegroom. The greatest solution for breaking that stronghold of fear is having God's love in our heart expelling the darkness of the lies. The mighty weapon of our prayer language can also be used to penetrate the wickedness and declare war against powers and lies that have been released in hopes of affecting our choices and ultimately your destiny.

Love conquers all. Love dispels jealousy. Love kills fear. Love drives back religious spirits. The love of God says, "Trust Me for I am God and I am in you in the battle."

God needs those who are willing to be as Gideon and trust Him to win their battle. This is how to advance God's Kingdom on the earth and agree with the divine plan of Heaven. God's army is required to arise in courage without fear.

In Judges 7:2-3 we see Gideon leading the Israelites against the Midianites. God told him that he had too many people with him; therefore, the number of them must be reduced so they would know that it was God who had delivered the victory into their hands. God told Gideon to proclaim to the men that if they were fearful and afraid to return to their homes. There were 22,000 men who chose to leave. The war was won because they believed God and believed that Gideon was God's man for the battle.

Fear is our worst enemy and it is a demonic one. If we have fear issues inside, in our heart and mind, then we cannot fight the good fight of faith. Faith and fear cannot exist together. The church for years has been avoiding warfare because the people have had no power with which to come against the principalities and powers of the enemy. We still don't have to listen very long before we hear their talk full of fear, doubt, and unbelief. They have not comprehended who they really are in Christ, kings and priests unto our God.

The enemy has used the spirit of fear in the church to block them from overcoming to see the people delivered and set free. The devil is the author of fear. It never comes from God. The devil is a liar. God has not given us the spirit of fear, but of power, love, and a sound mind. (See 2 Timothy 1:7.) Fear above all else is the worst enemy of the church. When we hear that little voice that says, "But what if I lose", that is the voice of the enemy and not of God. In God we are victorious in all things.

It is so important for us to learn to dwell in the secret place of the Most High according to Psalms 91. I believe this psalm reveals God's heart in spiritual warfare and is God's voice sounding from Heaven. I believe the Lord of hosts, the Lion of the Tribe of Judah is roaring over the United States and Israel. He who dwells in the secret place (He is constantly dwelling) – in the position of the Spirit – is in a place of conquering. God is always there, not wandering aimlessly. He that is in position in the secret place of the Most High is staying in the creative power of God (in His shadow). Everything comes down to being under the shadow of God when we position ourselves in heavenly places.

We must take time to dwell in God. There is no place for fearful words to be spoken, no room for confusion or a mixed message. We should only be affected by one voice the voice of God. We resist the fear that others may try to bring to us. We must learn to tolerate zero fear.

God's voice sounds like a mighty army. It is not by merely quoting scriptures that we win, but by dwelling – abiding – in the Word of God. It is only from this position of being in Christ – being one with Him – that we consistently hear the voice of God and experience His love manifested through our lives.

I John 4:17-21:

> *"17 Herein is our love made perfect, that we may have boldness in the Day of Judgment: because as he is, so are we in this world. 18 There is no fear in love; but perfect love castes out fear: because fear hath torment. He that feared is not made perfect in love. 19 We love him, because he first loved us. 20 If a man says, I love God, and hated his brother, he is a liar: for he that loves not his brother whom he hath seen, how can he love God whom he hath not seen? 21 And this commandment has we from him, That he who loves God love his brother also."*

We must each recognize the fact that fears is our personal worst enemy. We are told to be bold. Only love makes us bold. Every battle is a judgment trial in heavenly places. God declares judgment over His enemy. The devil is our accuser and tries to convict us in the courtroom before God. Win your case. Make your choice to win it. That is why it is so important to let God perfect His love dwell within us.

It is important to be perfected in love before a battle. Fear concentrates on who we are. Love is the opposite. Through love we are willing to give our lives. Thus, we know that we have love when we lay down our lives for others. Love is a giver; fear is a taker.

LOVE is the opposite – we are willing to give your life. Thus we know love that we lay down our lives for our friend.

In the church today we must be careful not to be a church of fearful takers. What can I receive? What will God give me today? Pastor, feed me. Bless me or I will leave. These attitudes are not based in the love of God, but in fear. The devil takes from them daily. He who keeps his life loses it. He who gives will preserve his life. Fear always puts us in the territory of the enemy.

It is very helpful and clarifying to realize that love is not a decision. Rather, Love is a person – Jesus! The Gospel says that love is a person in Jesus Christ who wants to live in us. God wants to hear us say, "I put You above everything and everyone else in my life. Take my life, Lord, and use it for Your glory."

To be a disciple of the Lord is to love and not hate. Jesus is not about holding in, but about giving. The real battle is about love! And the real battle is on. All around us are those who are desperate to experience God's unconditional love flowing through us to them.

It wounded the Father's heart when Adam and Eve listened to the voice of the devil, and in one split second, the whole family of God was taken away. That wound spoke immediately and still says, "I want them back." Is there someone who will wage battle for them? Yes, I say yes, Lord. Jesus paid an incredible price for us. How can we do less than give Him our all and follow His plan and path for our lives?

Commitment and perseverance is what it takes. Blood is calling from the lands from all around the earth. Who will take what the devil stole from us and bring it back? Perfect love is a giver, not a selfish taker. Real love produces the desire and the ability to bless others, void of any motive of personal gain. Real love says simply, "What can I do for You, Lord?"

In contrast, fear is a spirit that strives to control humanity by force. Fear is always from the enemy and is designed to stop your destiny. Satan will attempt to stop every right decision needed in God's plan for you to be fruitful and multiply.

Fear has so many voices, so many questions, so many premeditated scenarios to play through the mind. Fear will try to tell us not to stand up in our church and walk in love or move in our gifting. But God says He will pour out His Spirit. Fear will tell us we're going to be sick, we're going to run out of supplies and money, we're going to be alone, we're going to die. The list of fear's messages is a long and horrible one.

But God is love; God is trustworthy. He has promised to never us nor forsake us. He has promised in His love for us to supply our every need, to always provide healing and abundance of life. As we walk by faith in the knowledge of these truths God's love will be perfected within us. Simply, where there is still fear, the love of God has not yet been fully perfected.

One thing Satan could never do is touch the Love of God. It is off limits to him. Our being filled with the love of God is our greatest defense in battle! God is the only source of this love. In Him we live and move and have my being.

Right now I offer this prayer for you, my reader, to be filled love and free of fear. Lord, I ask that all manner of fear be cast down in this one's life now and bound to the feet of Jesus. I ask that faith come and fill their vessel. Grant them faith to move mountains of fear in others' lives and in the church. Lord, I ask that Your liquid love be poured out from Your heart to theirs so they may know Your unconditional agape love is true, real and manifesting through them as they follow Your ways and your will. In Jesus' name we pray. Amen.

CHAPTER 7:

Great Grace Awakening

Just what is grace? To most of us who hear the word so often, do we really know what it means? According to Nelson's Illustrated Bible Dictionary the definition of grace is "favor or kindness shown without regard to the worth or merit of the one who receives it and in spite of what that same person deserves. Grace is one of the key attributes of God. The Lord God is 'merciful and gracious, long-suffering, and abounding in goodness and truth' (Ex 34:6). Therefore, grace is almost always associated with mercy, love, compassion, and patience as the source of help and with deliverance from distress."

When I was in Europe, specifically Ireland and France, God told me He was going to release His great grace and awaken His church, that He is releasing His horses to patrol the earth, and therefore, for me to get ready to run with the horses of the Kingdom.

Let Him release deeper revelation of His plan and His word into your heart. It will taste like honey to your spirit and open your eyes as you seek Him. Honey pours out of the rock in Psalm 85. The Rock is Jesus and the honey is revelation and nourishment to sustain us with His Word. Jonathon ate honey and his eyes were open during the battle with the Philistines. Saul had told his men not to eat from the land and they obeyed and became weak. But Jonathan did not hear the command and fed on the honey and suddenly understood the outcome of the battle. So I believe God is saying to those who are the remnant that His Word will have a fresh honeycomb flavor, seasoned with deep revelation. We will learn much from God as we meditate on the Word of God.

He is calling the church to arise as kings and priests and stand in intercession for justice, righteousness, truth and holiness. He is saying, "Grace, grace, grace to the mountain of obstacles in your life and your household." He is calling for those mountains to be moved out of the way so that we can pursue His destiny for our life.

Right now, take hold of this word and speak to the mountains in your life – in your soul, your mind, your will – and be loosed from the fear, doubt, and unbelief that is besetting you. Some of us may go through the mountain and some of us over it with hind's feet on high places, but we have the authority in Christ to speak to the mountain to be removed (Read Mark 11:22-24).

While ministering in the city of Honfleur in France I felt led to share my testimony. So I began sharing being raised as a Lutheran and graduating from 2 year Catechism class, taking my first communion in front of the church and confessing my believe in Christ according to the Apostles Creed. However, I was instructed by the best but I was spiritually dead on the inside. There is a heart change that needs to take place. My mind knew of Christ but I had not applied the truths to my heart, my life for daily living and so I was a weak Christian when temptation came.

It took much more grace from God to lead me to deliverance and inner healing to see and admit what Christ really did for me on the cross at Calvary repenting for the seven deadly sins of the church in scripture: non-Christian activities, deception, unforgiveness, pride, rebellion, bondage, and ancestral curses. Many bible studies later and a loving touch from God to include personal prophecies compelled me to seek Him more and more.

I believe my life is an example of God's mercy and an extension of His grace. I have been forgiven of so much and now I walk in a new dimension of faith, hope, and love for others. At the end of my testimony I heard the Lord ask me to call the youth forward. When I did His fire fell on them and they lay prostrate on the floor.

Who is carrying the "new fire" anointing? It has been evident to me in the ministry that it is those who are saying, yes, to the Lord and running to His altar to know Him. Their surrender in humility to serve Him becomes the conduit of power and they are becoming ministers of holy fire. They are God's remnant reserved to carry His glory. They are getting free from the snares of the world and are emerging with power. They are enduring the persecution and false accusations thrown at them by the enemy. They are being refined in God's fire. They are totally sold out to God's ways. They are right with God and God intercedes for them.

Their ability to honor others and work with a team increases their authority and effectiveness. They are not afraid to share their testimony. They are not afraid to tell of God's grace toward them because they are not ashamed of the gospel of Christ. For them it has truly become the power of God for salvation. This anointing breaks the hold of the enemy in every way and even cultural differences are freed through the word of their testimony and the ever-increasing revelation of His blood.

They are not hiding in caves. They are leaders taking lands, tribes, and unreached groups of people. They are filled with a holy boldness born of being one who is loved and favored by God. They are called by His name, born to inherit nations, born specifically for this hour of history.

These have laid down the weapons of carnal warfare, trading them in for revelation of God's extreme love and strategy from Heaven. God spoke so clearly that a great awakening was coming to the United States and spilling over to Ireland and then to France and flowing down across the Middle East. He said to me before I left for the journey (He has such a sense of humor, I believe), "Did you know – and tell them so – I cannot be killed, and try as they may throughout the generations of time. Attempts have been made on My life, but I cannot be killed; nor can you...or you...for we have eternal life and you will rule and reign with Me for all eternity!"

The Lord went on to tell me to tell them that this lie is so temporary compared to all He has for us and not to treasure this world, but to receive His love and grace to win the lost. It is foolish, isn't it; to think they can kill God or us. God is the "I am" and "the Spirit and Truth." Nothing can kill God. Nothing can truly kill us as children of God.

Are you born again? Do you know that He knows who you are, where you live? God wants to express His love on the earth. Are you doing that or has the enemy hardened your heart or put false yokes on you to hold back the compassion of Christ in you?

I believe that the intercessors will carry the day and call in the move of God. Do you want to be a part of that move? Do you want to usher in the glorious realm of the Kingdom of God? Zechariah 4:6 NKJV says, 'Not by might nor by power, but by My Spirit,' says the Lord of hosts. God's Holy Spirit needs to flow once again like a mighty river in the church. There needs to be a lighthouse pointing people to Christ. God is giving us a strategy for taking this city, for surrounding the city with prayer cells and capturing those crying out in the wilderness, bringing them to Jesus. We must ask God for increase in revelation and strategy for taking the stronghold of religion and for a complete release of the funds with which to do it.

Are you aware that grace is present to assist you in the very things God has called you to do? Angels will come to you. Love and joy will be flowing from you. You only have to ask. Angels came to me in Austria when I needed refreshing. It was incredible! One on each arm ministered supernatural life-giving strength to me from Heaven.

Someone walked up to me once and said, "God calls you His dove of love." Jonah's name means dove and he was called to lead people to repentance for it is the key to knowing God's unconditional love and grace. People around us need to see His love and grace in us through the lives we live. Oh how God loves His church.

We must move forward in this our calling by faith. Faith is accompanied by hope which is a confident expectation. Hope brings deliverance and deliverance brings new freedom.

John 20:21-23:

> *"[21] Then said Jesus to them again, Peace is unto you: as my Father hath sent me, even so send I you. [22] And when he had said this, he breathed on them, and said unto them, Receive ye the Holy Ghost: [23] who's so ever sins ye remit, they are remitted unto them; and who's so ever sins ye retain, they are retained."*

Jesus released His disciples to go and forgive others and breathed on them the Holy Spirit. Has God breathed fresh on you lately? Jesus on the cross breathed His last breath on the centurion and he proclaimed that truly, this is the Son of God. (See Mark 15:37-39.) It is now the hour not to be silent, but to proclaim Christ. Grace is the action of God's favor upon His people. We are destined for favor. It is unmerited divine assistance given to humans for their regeneration or sanctification.

Today like never before we are all faced with days of great uncertainty. It is so easy for moments of fear to creep into our minds. Because of this, we have seen God's grace coming to us, changing us, depositing within us more faith and assistance from above.

You can use the angelic host and dispatch them into the enemy's camp. You will be glad you called upon the ministering and warring angels to deliver your family, your city, your country. They are there for you. Believe and ask God for signs, wonders and miracles to take place in your life, in your ministry. God uses His angels to work for you. That is their purpose.

I personally believe that God would have us His children, even in these challenging times, to learn to laugh and rest in Him. We need to lighten up at times. The presence of God and of His angels is a delight in my life. So welcome them into your own life. I believe you will fully enjoy your experiences with God and with the angels.

This great love and grace might just be the very thing you have been asking Papa God for. Activation of His grace is shed abroad in our hearts. Each of us has been chosen by our Lord to promote His agenda of great grace to the world. We all carry a quality of grace that permits the Holy Spirit's grace to fall upon us.

Today if you will, accept and expect a deposit of this grace right now. Just receive it by faith into your spirit. It is freely given by He who is Grace. Right now, be free, be released. Let go of all self-condemnation, accusations, and guilt. Don't allow the religious spirits to rob you of this grace or of your freedom in Christ. Keep your eyes on this grace; refuse to lose sight of it. The Galatian believers lost sight and they became bewitched into believing lies from the enemy about the true gospel of Christ. In Galatians 5:22-23 we learn that the fruit of the Spirit is love, joy, peace, long-suffering, gentleness, goodness, faith, meekness, and temperance. Pray both in the Spirit and with your understanding. Let the joy of His river bubble up within you and release a new song to minister unto your King.

Genesis 39:4:

> *"And Joseph found grace in his sight, and he served him: and he made him overseer over his house and that entire he had he put into his hand."*

Ephesians 4:7:

> *"But unto every one of us is given grace according to the measure of the gift of Christ."*

Expecting a new encounter with the holy laughter and joy of the Lord will help us receive the dimension of the Holy Spirit to walk and live in grace as a way of life. Zephaniah 3:17 NIV tells us:

> *"The Lord your God is with you, the Mighty Warrior who saves. He will take great delight in you; in His love He will no longer rebuke you, but will rejoice over you with singing."*

Let the Lord water the seed of joy over you. Lord, we ask you to seed the atmosphere with Your joy. Thank You that Your people will be satisfied with You. Thank You that Your presence is enough for all. We give You praise, Lord God, for You alone are worthy to be praised.

I would ask you, dear reader, to examine yourself. Are you included in the remnant to carry God's grace in the eleventh hour of the church age? The remnant wins. God would say to you, "I am with you to deliver you from the wicked and from the terrible hands of the mockers in the spiritual realm. Obey My commands and I will do this."

To follow in this walk of obedience and ministry is to live a separated life unto the Lord. It may change the people we are able to hang out with. It will call us to flow in His love toward everyone we encounter regardless of how we may be treated back. We will yield ourselves up to be God's voice on the earth. We will probably be asked to do things for Him that are outside our comfort zone.

CHAPTER 8:

Healing River of His Love

There is much spoken today on the topic of love, so many words, in fact, that it is easy to lose sight of love's true meaning. The world has its own definitions, its own way of thinking, believing, and acting on this thing called love. But as is the case in so many other areas of life, the world's ways and God's ways are not even close to the same. Love is definitely one of those topics in which the world's view misses God's view is unconditional.

God's river of love is very real and runs through His Kingdom. There is healing in the river and revelations of all kinds. In the book of Ezekiel, chapter 47, the prophet talks about God's river. We have experienced a heavenly flow.

While in Jerusalem at the All Nations Convocation prayer watch, God gave me a word of knowledge that someone needed God's healing touch. As I shared what God was telling me, the leader raised his hand that it was him. Praying for him the healing river of God manifested and he was in the river. God heard his heart cry to be healed and he was.

Apostle John is often referred to as the apostle of love. His writings teach much about the love of God for us. He also wrote much about our responses to the love of God as well. In his day, there were many heresies that tried to dilute or dissolve the truth concerning the love of God. If the enemy could do away with or lessen the potency of God's love in the hearts of man he would have a stronghold from which to destroy. In John 10:10 the same apostle wrote, "The thief comes not, but for to steal, and to kill, and to destroy: I have come that they might have life, and that they might have it more abundantly." There has always been an ongoing war waged by the devil against the love of God within ourselves, our relationships and the church.

Satan's plan to destroy our view and experience of God's love is so important to him that he fights its flow constantly; I believe it's worth our time and effort to see what God really has to say about it. I believe it is imperative that we come to know God according to His love.

The Bible teaches us that God is not merely a God whose character is one of love. He is one who has a great love for everyone. He is not like us; we are created to be like Him, in His image. This is true but we must be transformed to act Godly. For instance, I am a loving person. I'm nice, kind, gentle. I can be fun to be with; I can be strong and confronting when necessary. That's all good. But if pushed far enough, I can get out of love. All of a sudden, given the right circumstances and provocations, my reaction can turn immediately into something hateful, hurtful, less than loving. Perfecting love in us is God's job so that we act Godly flowing in grace.

God, however, is not merely a loving God. The Bible tells us that God IS love. He can only do love. He can only say love. He can only be love. Even when He must bring judgment and correction, they are still based in love. It is love that does not allow evil to go on forever. And it is love that saves us, love that fills us with the Holy Spirit, love that heals us and protects us. God is completely love and He never changes. We cannot push His buttons until He falls out of love with us. Jesus paid the price for all the sins of the world forever on the cross. What a rich heritage is ours as born-again children of God to show the power and price of love.

1 John 4:4-19:

"4 Ye are of God, little children, and have overcome them: because greater is he that is in you, than he that is in the world. 5 They are of the world: therefore speak them of the world, and the world hears them. 6 We are of God: he that knows God hears us; he that is not of God hears not us. Hereby know us the spirit of truth, and the spirit of error.

7 Beloved, let us love one another: for love is of God; and every one that loves is born of God, and knows God. 8 He that loves not knows not God; for God is love. 9 In this was manifested the love of God toward us, because that God sent his only begotten Son into the world, that we might live through him. 10 Herein is love, not that we loved God, but that he loved us, and sent his Son to be the propitiation for our sins. 11 Beloved, if God so loved us, we ought also to love one another. 12 No man hath seen God at any time. If we love one another, God dwelled in us, and his love is perfected in us. 13 Hereby know we that we dwell in him, and he in us, because he hath given us of his Spirit. 14 And we have seen and do testify that the Father sent the Son to be the Savior of the world. 15 Whosoever shall confess that Jesus is the Son of God, God dwelled in him, and he in God. 16 And we have known and believed the love that God hath to us. God is love; and he that dwelled in love dwelled in God and God in him. 17 Herein is our love made perfect, that we may have boldness in the Day of Judgment: because as he is, so are we in this world. 18 There is no fear in love; but perfect love casts out fear: because fear hath torment. He that fears is not made perfect in love. [19] We love him, because he first loved us."

So since we have such a rich heritage of unconditional love from our Father, why are so many in the body of Christ not experiencing that love more fully? There are so many lonely hearts in the church, so many who feel rejected, abandoned, lonely with little or no sense of the Father's deep abiding love for them personally.

The answer lies partly in the world around us. It's difficult, if not impossible, to turn on a television today and watch a current program, supposedly designed for entertainment, without getting bombarded with the enemy's negative view of just about everything. Profanity and innuendo abound as do every sexual vice and deviance that comes to mind. Divorce is presented as the natural side-effect of marriage. Every other commercial tells of another disease and a drug to fight it along with a list of horrible potential side-effects of taking the cure. Poverty and crime abound. News broadcasts are filled with seemingly more and more violent acts. Fear knocks on every door to the point where neighbors are strangers to each other now. Where is God's love in the midst of all this?

In James 1:17 we are told:

"Every good gift and every perfect gift is from above, and cometh down from the Father of lights, with who is no variableness, neither shadow of turning."

In God there is no variation or shadow of turning. This is telling us that God doesn't change. He doesn't love us one day and hate us the next. His love is unfailing toward us every second of every day and beyond. When time is done away and we move on, His love will still be the same for us – utterly complete, totally saturating.

"Forever, O Lord, thy word is settled in heaven." – Psalm 119:89

"Thy word is a lamp unto my feet, and a light unto my path." – Psalm 119:105

God intends on our experiencing – living in moment-to-moment – His great all-consuming love. The most profound blessing our spirit needs to receive...and can receive...is the father-heart of God. We must come to a place by faith of knowing His special creation of us, His kind intention toward us, His matchless love for us, and His glory revealed in us. The resurrection power of Christ is actively available to our spirits and is working on our behalves to set us free. How our Father longs to see us living in the fullness of His love, soaring on eagles' wings above this present darkness. His plan has never changed. The darkness cannot put out the light.

Blessing our spirit through prayer is an amazing way to heal by letting our spirit man takes over the healing process. We believe that since we are born again by the Spirit of God we can ask the same Spirit to heal our emotions, our minds, our hearts, and our bodies.

As our spirit man is enlarged by God's power through His Word and as we continue to speak His Word, we will come to know Him more and more. We will come to experience Him personally rather than just know things about Him. The difference is life-changing.

This truth is what King David knew. He had become a giant killer because his spirit man was of giant proportion. David chose to believe the will and covenant of God over all the circumstances that looked bigger than anything! He knew his God. His faith and strength didn't come from knowing about God. David knew Him intimately and well. God had prepared him to confront the giant. God had taught him many things when he was a mere boy tending sheep. David knew in his heart God had prepared him for that day.

I have found that it is in the reaching out by faith to grasp and receive the love God has for me that I find a healing balm. As I apply His love to my life by faith, I experience healing within, a breaking out from the lies I have believed about God, myself and others. Sometimes healing comes in an instant and that is a wonderful gift of God. But so many times our healing comes a little piece at a time as we continue to allow His love to enter our hearts, minds, and emotions.

It is so important to fill our eyes with the promises of God's love and healing in His Word. Isaiah 53:4-5 tells us Jesus paid for our healing – spirit, soul, and body. 1 Peter 2:24 tells us that by His stripes we were healed. There are so many scriptures that tell us this very truth. The same is true of His love. John 3:16 is profound when we stop to think. The God of the whole creation loves US so much that He gave His only Son in order to bring us back to life everlasting in Him. I don't know a parent who would sacrifice his child for the whole world – that world that doesn't even appreciate or receive what was done. But God did it. And Jesus came willingly. That is total love! Yes, we must fill our eyes with the truth of God's love and healing. I can personally testify to the miraculous healing in my own body from 18 allergies to 5; losing 70 lbs. from looking on the inside of my own beliefs about myself; stability of emotions and responding in love to the lost versus indifference and apathy.

We must fill our ears with His love for us, too. These are vitally important steps to walking above the darkness and hopelessness of the world. Things are very bright and good in the Kingdom of God. There are wonderful ministers singing healing music that touches deep within the heart and soul. The blessing of sound reaches very deeply within us to the molecular cell level. God can and will use music like this to bring about a healing change within us.

Another very important thing for us to learn to flow in is worship of our loving God. I have seen a spiritual treasure chest filled with glorious gems of God's wisdom and blessings when I worship Him.

John 4:23:

> *"But the hour comes and now is, when the true worshippers shall worship the Father in spirit and in truth: for the Father seeks such to worship him."*

God desires to fill us with His love, to heal us, to bless us. We get to yield ourselves to Him, surrendering to His unconditional love. Allow Him to open the treasure of His healing and wisdom to you. Let Him reveal to your spirit who you are in Christ, how God sees you. Receiving by faith truths of your true identity in Him brings healing.

Many of us entertain hopelessness, powerlessness, or despair thoughts- a familiar victim mentality. That is what the enemy of our soul has told us to do; it's all we deserve according to the devil. But when we receive the truth of God by the anointing of the Holy Spirit, everything changes. God says that we are over-comers by the words of our testimony releasing joy, hope, love and wholeness. It's really not about what we might deserve. God's love for us is a gift, undeserved, unmerited, but completely freely given to each of us.

When I was baptized with the Holy Spirit and began to come into the reality of this, I was literally euphoric for hours. I was overwhelmed by the love of God. It was marvelous...and it still is. All I did was ask for Him. I said something like, "God, if you are real, then I want to know you. I want You to lead, guide and direct me into restoration and healing." I had no idea how wounded and cursed I was until Jesus touched me and made me whole.

The Power of the Blessing

The Hebrew has practiced the power of blessing each Friday night at Shabbat at sundown for centuries. Their success in the world reveals the power of the blessing. The husband and wife bless each other and then they turn and bless their children verbally 52 times a year.

Sylvia Gunter and Arthur Burk discovered the power of the blessing for this generation. They wrote a book, Blessing Your Spirit, which is a wonderful resource and tool to use.

One does not even realize how cursed they are until they are around people who have been living out the blessings of the promises of God for generations. It is amazing truth that we are awakening to in the church.

Someone who is blessed does not realize why someone would entertain lies about themselves. The mind is a very powerful thing and scriptures tell us to be transformed by the renewing of our minds. There is power in positive thinking!

> *"Therefore, I urge you brothers, in view of God's mercy, to offer your bodies as living sacrifices, holy and pleasing to God—this is your spiritual act of worship. Do not conform any longer to the pattern of this world, but be transformed by the renewing of your mind. Then you will be able to test and approve what God's will is—his good, pleasing and perfect will." – Romans 12:1-2*

When we hear a blessing spoken it resounds in our spirit in a profound way. Like a soaking in love we have not experienced or like receiving a truth for the very first time awakens us to a whole new world of creation, new sounds and the river of life. So many speak of this, but so few have found it. When we speak to our "slumbering spirit" to wake up and look up to see Father God, we become alive again.

"Being filled with the Spirit" means that God's Spirit infuses and controls your spirit, soul, and body. When your spirit is controlled by His Spirit and is dominant over your soul, your whole being is conformed to God's truth and His intention for your life.

What God has given you from His own essence is more than enough; it is where you are celebrated, where you are loved and where you are affirmed.

CHAPTER 9:

Jonah: Obedience is Key

Obedience is always the key to God's ways and it is up to us to trust God and put our faith in whatever He tells us to do. Recently, God asked me to take a large ornamental key off the wall in my office. He told me to stand and prophetically turn the key until He told me to stop. As I obeyed I was taken up in the spirit and saw myself, as Jonah, in a storm of life with turbulent waters raging all around. Then I was overboard in the water where the enemy wanted me, trapped by his evil spirits, similar to Jonah being swallowed and kept in the belly of the whale for 3 days. As I continued to turn the key God reached out and put me securely on the deck of the ship. I was covered in unclean things from the sea, from trying to minister to unclean people who really did not want God. Continuing to turn the key they fell off of me and I was clean again. Refreshed from the revelation and cleansing by God I continued to turn the key and thanked God for rescuing me from the assignment against me. This is obedience not humanism.

Then, I heard Him tell me to use this new prophetic tool: the turning of the key by faith to get a fresh revelation; in order to set others free from iniquities, assignments, addictions, trauma, and fears. He told me to be open to whatever God shows me and believes by faith what is revealed.

If we are walking with God or wanting to walk with God, He will often give us directions. It is not uncommon at all to hear something floating up in our hearts that we know is the voice of the Lord. It comes with clarity and immediate obedience to His direction is powerful. He means for us to do it now. This should be a normal experience to those walking with Him but not an everyday one. Walking with the Lord, challenges each and every one to have our spiritual ears in tuned with His voice so we do not miss His directions and wisdom.

And so it was with Jonah in the Old Testament. This short book of four simple chapters relates quite a powerful story for us to learn from today. God gave Jonah a simple direction in the first two verses. But it was his flesh that found it difficult to yield.

Jonah 1:1-2:

> *"1 Now the word of the Lord came unto Jonah the son of Amittai, saying, 2 Arise, go to Nineveh, that great city, and cry against it; for their wickedness is come up before me."*

That's pretty clear. Now Nineveh was "an exceeding great city" that lay on the Tigris River. It was built originally by Nimrod, and due to its geographic position, was a great trade route between the Mediterranean and Indian Oceans. It was a city – a people – filled with much wickedness. God was preparing to bring judgment to them and thus wanted Jonah to go to them first and tell them to repent or suffer the consequences.

In the very next verse we see Jonah's surprising response to this request from God. Jonah didn't tell God, "Okay. I'll go do what you told me. Let me get my bags packed and off I go. Thanks for wanting to use me in this way, Lord."

Jonah 1:3:

> *"But Jonah rose up to flee unto Tar shish from the presence of the Lord, and went down to Joppa; and he found a ship going to Tar shish: so he paid the fare*

thereof, and went down into it, to go with them unto Tar shish from the presence of the Lord."

No. Instead of running toward obedience, Jonah – this man of God – fled the other direction. He was actually trying to get away from the very presence of God. So much so that he bought a ticket and boarded a ship and headed out of town in the wrong direction.

But we know that it is pointless to try to run away from God. He who never leaves us or forsakes us always knows right where we are and why and what we're doing there! And Jonah was to learn that lessen well himself soon enough. The ship hit a storm and the ship came into such peril that even Jonah admitted that he was the one at fault. So he told them to throw him overboard and the seas were calmed.

We probably all know the story of how the big fish swallowed up poor Jonah and how he was held there in that awful place. Eventually Jonah prayed and repented for his disobedience, finally choosing to thank his God. In the end Jonah told the Lord he would now go on to Nineveh and be obedient to what God had told him to do in the first place. And the fish tossed him out onto the dry land.

Jonah 3:1-4:

"And the word of the Lord came unto Jonah the second time, saying, 2 Arise, go unto Nineveh, that great city, and preach unto it the preaching that I bid thee. 3 So Jonah arose, and went unto Nineveh, according to the word of the Lord. Now Nineveh was an exceeding great city of three days' journey. 4 And Jonah began to enter into the city a day's journey, and he cried, and said, yet forty days, and Nineveh shall be overthrown."

Although there are further and deeper messages within the rest of Jonah's Nineveh experience with God, let us for now just look at his act of disobedience. Don't you wonder what he was thinking, what emotions stirred up so quickly in him that apparently just moments after hearing the Lord tell him to go preach to Nineveh, he turned on his heel and went the other way. He didn't just put his hands in his pockets and tell God he'd think about it or he'd do it later. No, he ran to the nearest ship and booked immediate passage the other direction from Nineveh.

It's so easy to throw stones at Jonah from the vantage of hindsight. "Why didn't he just go there?" we might ask. Maybe no one really knows exactly what was going inside of Jonah's head and heard, but I believe that God was asking to do something that went against his own thinking.

Something we need to carry home to ourselves in Jonah's experience is that obedience to God means doing what He tells us without question or insertion of our own opinion. God really doesn't need our opinions in His knowing what to do and how to do it. He's got the plan well in hand without us. But He needs our willingness. He needs our hands and feet and voices. And that is a huge lesson for each of us to learn.

In a simple act of obedience, I took communion on the eve of Passover and 3 days later our adopted Korean daughter tried to commit suicide. Death was aborted. She was very angry. But God spared her life through a simple obedient act of hearing God.

What is true repentance?

Jonah and the prophet Jeremiah were both surrounded by much wickedness in their times. Unclean lives were all around. When involved in wickedness, there must be true repentance. When evil spirits are present, they must be driven out. I believe there are seven actions that are present in truly repentant person.

1. **They will break up their fallow ground. (Jeremiah 4:3)**
2. **Mourn with Godly sorrow over sin. (Jeremiah 9:17-18)**
3. **Pray for your country. (Jeremiah 36:7)**
4. **Love God's Word like honey. (Jeremiah 20)**
5. **Love others. (Jeremiah 31:3; John 13:34)**

6. **Share Jesus Christ. (Jeremiah 31:31; 33:1-9,15,17)**
7. **Rest in His will without fear; be obedient.**

There is a difference between Godly sorrow (repentance) and worldly sorrow. This is shown clearly in the following passage from Paul:

2 Corinthians 7:10:

> *"For Godly sorrow worked repentance to salvation not to be repented of: but the sorrow of the world worked death."*

The following comparison list will help you know that you are truly repentant of sin and not just going through the motions of the world:

Godly Sorrow

Work of the Holy Spirit; brings life.	We rise up to Christ in hope.
God defends me. (Psalm 54:1-5)	Victory in the wounding of Christ.
God's way is reward.	"God, come and heal me."
The blood of Christ is enough.	Hands lifted in surrender.
Confessing our own sin.	Crying out to God. (Psalm 28:1-2; 27:7-8)
Sorrow to God for my sins.	Running to God for help.
Seeing God's mercy in Jesus' wounds.	Hope of new life in resurrection.
Convicts me of sin. (Psalm 51)	Remembering all God has done.
My head lifts up. (Psalm 3:3, 4; 27:6)	Hidden in Christ.
Filled with hope of forgiveness.	Deep internal work by the Spirit.

Worldly Sorrow

Work of the enemy; brings death.

I defend myself.

My way is retaliation.

I want revenge my way.

Crying over what is done to me.

Sorrow for myself over sin.

See my own wounds only.

Condemnation – Judas.

Head hanging down.

Having no hope.

"God, why me? Why me?"

Hands lifted with clenched fists.

Complaining to man.

Running to man with woe.

Hopelessness and death.

Remembering me and my wound.

Hiding in my own sorrow.

False and shallow work of the flesh.

We sink into our own wound.

We sink down in hopelessness.

Repentance

Let us come back to the work of obedience. We can see plainly how true repentance differs from worldly sorrow. The book of Jonah tells us that, when in the belly of the fish, Jonah did truly repent. His experience of repenting came with great thankfulness to God. Right there while still in the belly of the fish repentance and thankfulness came across his lips. And God honored the words of his heart. He was immediately delivered up onto dry land. He was immediately restored.

Romans 6:16:

> *"Know ye not, that to whom ye yield yourselves servants to obey, his servants ye are to whom ye obey; whether of sin unto death, or of obedience unto righteousness?"*

To those of us who are determined to live our lives in the fullness of God's presence and blessing, it is imperative that we learn to obey with speed and great thankfulness. "Lord, what would You have me to do today?" should be the cry of our heart always. And when we hear His voice asking us to participate in His plan in some way, we must develop the willingness and courage to step up at once and say, "Yes, Lord. I will."

God is always reaching out to people on the earth – all the people on the earth – in an effort to bring them to His love, to salvation in His Son. That is always His heart. That was his heart in Nineveh when He told Jonah to go and speak to them. How God desired for them to turn from their evil, to repent and come to Him. Do you see that He must have Jonah's voice to go speak His word of warning to that people? Without a man working with Him, He would not reach these people.

It should be noted that once Jonah came to himself and finally went to Nineveh with God's message, the people heard him and received the message.

Jonah 3:5:

> *"So the people of Nineveh believed God, and proclaimed a fast, and put on sackcloth, from the greatest of them even to the least of them."*

From the greatest to the least of them, they all turned toward God. God worked through His man, Jonah, and accomplished what He wanted.

What has God asked you to do for Him today? Yesterday? This week? Are you ignoring His voice, His wishes? Truly God wants you to be part of His plan in the earth. There is so much to be done; He has plans for each and every one of us to help bring everything to completion. Don't ignore Him any longer. Let today...right now...be the turning point for you and your life. Pray this with me:

Lord, take my life and use me for Your will. Teach me Your ways. Tell me today what You want me to do. Give me directions and I will obey You. Thank You for loving me and for wanting to work with me in Your plans for this earth. I yield myself to You now, Lord. I receive it done by faith now. Thank you Lord.

If you prayed this prayer just now expect, God to speak to your heart. Anticipate Him speaking to you in your prayer times, in your time in His Word. Pray and make yourself available to Him to speak into your heart. You will recognize that it is Him. You may not like what He tells you, but you will recognize His voice. And be quick to obey. Jump and run when He tells you where to go and what to do. He will be with you every step of the way and you will see Him move on people by His Spirit. You will see His mighty plan for the earth unfold. You will be a part of it.

CHAPTER 10:

Steps to Restoration: God's Plan

From the beginning, God's only plan for us has been to restore us. All that was lost in the fall through Adam's sin, Jesus redeemed back for us through His death, burial and resurrection. For us to settle for anything less along the way is never His will for us. Still, He did create us with the power of choice. He gave us a will of our own.

What does restoration mean? A look into most any dictionary will define it as to bring back from a former, original, or normal condition; to bring back to a state of health, soundness, or vigor; to put back to a former place, or to a former position or rank.

The provision has been made for us to live in abundance of life, goodness, blessing, health, joy, peace, prosperity. Jesus has provided everything for us when He became the curse for us. In Galatians 3:13 we read:

"Christ hath redeemed us from the curse of the law, being made a curse for us: for it is written, Cursed is every one that hanged on a tree:"

God has provided us His way to experience restoration in every area of our lives – spirit, soul, and body. This is not only true in the individual, but is equally true in the church. When we accept Jesus as our Savior and are born-again, our spirit is restored – made a new. What a wonderful miracle that is.

2 Corinthians 5:17:

"Therefore if any man be in Christ, he is a new creature: old things are passed away; behold all things are become new."

Likewise, as we have discussed earlier, Jesus also paid for our physical healing. Peter tells us that "by His stripes we were healed." We can claim these promises as ours and take them by faith, believing and thanking God for His awesome love for us.

Another area of our lives that God has promised full restoration in is the area of our soul. The soul is made up of the mind, the will, and the emotions. This is a huge and sometimes seemingly complicated part of us. What we think, what we feel, what we decide about everything are all seated in the soul. I like what David wrote in the 23rd Psalm:

"1 The Lord is my shepherd; I shall not want.

2 He makes me to lie down in green pastures: He leaded me beside the still waters.

3 He restores my soul: He leaded me in the paths of righteousness for his name's sake.

[4] Yea, though I walk through the valley of the shadow of death, I will fear no evil: for thou art with me; thy rod and thy staff they comfort me.

[5] Thou prepares a table before me in the presence of mine enemies: thou anoints my head with oil; my cup runs over.

[6] Surely goodness and mercy shall follow me all the days of my life: and I will dwell in the house of the Lord forever."

Note that verse three tells us that He restores our soul. God through Jesus and the Holy Spirit brings restoration to our mind, our will, and our emotions. All the fears and negative hurtful thoughts, all the mental anguish, depression, and pain are covered in God's promise of restoration. That means we do not have to live with these terrible things that work so hard to steal our peace and joy.

As is true with all the promises of God, there is a part we must play in order to walk in the full benefit of what He has provided for us. Just like in salvation, Jesus has provided eternal life for us, but we must do our part by believing on Him and confessing that He is the Son of God raised from the dead for us. In order to walk in that provision we must obey His Word concerning it.

One important step in restoration is to trust God. The Bible has much to say about trusting Him.

Psalm 5:11-12:

"[11] But let all those that put their trust in thee rejoice: let them ever shout for joy, because thou defends them: let them also that love thy name be joyful in thee. [12] For thou, Lord, wilt bless the righteous; with favor wilt thou compass him as with a shield."

Proverbs 3:5-6:

> *"[5] Trust in the Lord with all thine heart; and lean not unto thine own understanding.[6] In all thy ways acknowledge him,and he shall direct thy paths."*

Trust goes hand-in-hand with faith. In order to experience God's restoration we must accept it by faith. In Hebrews 11:6 we learn that without faith, it is impossible to please Him because we must believe that He is God and that He rewards those who seek Him diligently. If it is not possible to please God without faith, then we must walk in faith in order to receive anything of Him.

Another key to restoration is walking in forgiveness. In Mark 11:25-26 Jesus Himself tells us,

> *"[25] And when ye stand praying, forgive, if ye ought against any: that your Father also which is in heaven may forgive you your trespasses. [26] But if ye do not forgive, neither will your Father which is in heaven forgive your trespasses."*

Again in Matthew 18:21-22 we find a conversation about forgiveness that took place between Peter and Jesus.

> *"[21] Then came Peter to him, and said, Lord, how oft shall my brother sin against me, and I forgive him? Till seven times? [22] Jesus said unto him, I say not unto thee, until seven times: but, until seventy times seven."*

Forgiving others is not about condoning the bad things they have done. It is not excusing them. To the contrary, forgiveness is about our walking free from the bondage that the enemy tries to hold us in through that pain. Forgiveness is saying, "I'm choosing to give this pain to the Lord and I'm walking away from the harm you tried to do to me. I am choosing freedom over bondage." True forgiveness is a choice, not a feeling. We forgive by faith. And God honors that faith every time. Forgiveness is a huge step in the walk of restoration.

We are to walk in love as well. In the book of Revelation, Jesus warns us to not forsake our first love. Do you remember how wonderful it was right after you were born-again? There was such a sense of newness and life and love. Jesus is just about all you can think about! But slowly over time, that fire of first love burns down. Life happens. We get busy. Other things take over that place that He once held.

1 John 4:18-21:

> *"18 There is no fear in love; but perfect love casts out fear: because fear hath torment. He that fears is not made perfect in love. 19 We love him, because he first loved us. 20 If a man says, I love God, and hated his brother, he is a liar: for he that loves not his brother whom he hath seen, how can he love God whom he hath not seen? 21 And these commandments have we from him, that he who loves God loves his brother also."*

We must be willing to yield ourselves to Him completely. God created us with a will, a freedom of choice. To have made us any other way would have been to make us robots. He desires for us to choose to love Him, choose to fellowship Him, and choose to draw near to Him. There is a certain persecution that will come into our lives when we decide to follow Jesus in this close intimate walk. The world didn't receive Him and it doesn't receive us either. But we find true life by yielding ourselves to Him, denying ourselves, and walking with Him closely.

Matthew 16:24-25:

> *"24 Then said Jesus unto His disciples, If any man will come after me, let him deny himself, and take up his cross, and follow me. 25 For whosoever will save his life shall lose it: and whosoever will lose his life for my sake shall find it."*

One of the most powerful steps in the walk of restoration is that of humility. We have an excellent picture of it recorded by James.

James 4:6-10:

> *"[6] But he giveth more grace. Wherefore he said, God resisted the proud, but giveth grace unto the humble. [7] Submit you therefore to God. Resist the devil, and he will flee from you. [8] Draw nigh to God, and he will draw nigh to you. Cleanse your hands, ye sinners; and purify your hearts, ye double minded. [9] Be afflicted, and mourn, and weep: let your laughter be turned to mourning, and your joy to heaviness. [10] Humble yourselves in the sight of the Lord, and he shall lift you up."*

Proverbs 29:23:

> *"A man's pride shall bring him low: but honor shall uphold the humble in spirit."*

What blocks Restoration of the Soul?

Pride is a big deal with God. He hates it. He resists the proud. Pride can sneak in so easily sometimes we don't even realize we're caught in its trap. It in itself is deception to the greatest magnitude. We must be vigilant to humble ourselves before the Lord always. It is a wonderful thing when we do this and experience being lifted up by Him.

Maybe you would say, "I'm doing all these things and I still don't feel restored in my soul. I'm not experiencing that refreshing and newness in Him. What's wrong with me?" Times come when we stop and look at ourselves, take inventory, and realize we're coming up short of what God has promised us. It's good to realize where we are in our walk with the Lord. And there are reasons why restoration can be blocked.

Pride is the biggest offender. A sense of pride can cause us to resist God and others without realizing that's what we're doing. Emotions can hide within the façade of pride. Destroying the pride by humbling ourselves before God opens the way for God to minister to our souls in very deep and life-changing ways. Dealing with pride will perpetuate healing and ministry and, conversely, not dealing with pride when it is present will block any step of restoration. Pride thrusts us further into the kingdom of Satan as well as fear, doubt, and unbelief and utter destruction and division.

These areas of unexamined resistance toward God or man create barriers that break down unity within the body of Christ. It is true that unity within the Body can only come to the degree that we are healed and walking in wholeness.

These resistances can be caused by any number of internal issues that may be going on within us. Very often the root of them comes down to one or more of the following:

1. **Wounds and hurts that are not dealt with.**
2. **Sins that lies unconfessed within.**
3. **Unbroken iniquities.**
4. **Unforgiveness.**
5. **Demonic oppression.**

An unexamined resistance will follow a downward progression until unity is broken. What begins as coldness in manner deteriorates into aloofness and resentment. Judgment and criticism soon follow. These lead to a lack of confidence and trust which, in turn, leads to a lack of fellowship. Soon to follow is a lack of love and the end result is the lack of unity among the brethren.

We must check ourselves often for humility. God is raising up peacemakers in this hour. In my city our church went through a very difficult time; we needed healing. At one point the leadership called in a neutral specialist (a peacemaker) who interviewed each person in the congregation (500 people) over a two-year period. Through the process the people were taught on how to get back to our first love, Jesus. It took the entire two year span of time to steer the ship back on course, but it was worth the time and effort.

There was so much offense within the body at that time. Love had turned quite cold. We did not get a new pastor until the breakthrough and release came and healing was evident. Love was once again flowing and expressed. It was a very serious breach that had occurred. Unforgiveness and slander were quite strong. Hatred, not love, prevailed for a season. Satan's death assignment to take out the church was evident.

But...God's wisdom – God's Word – prevailed and the elders and others saw the error of their ways after much fasting, prayer, and heart searching. No one could have brought the church back to center but God. The skills and leadership of the trained specialist in facilitating reconciliation and restoration were required. Under that guidance we learned to forgive one another and come together in love. What Satan meant for evil, God turned back to good through our obedience and yielding.

The desire of God's heart is unity and love among the members of the body. The world is meant to know and recognize us by our love for one another. Offense is a wicked thing. Blessed are those who are "unoffended" in Jesus.

Restoration reminds us of Jesus. He restored us back to the union with God by sending a savior and then the savior sent the Holy Spirit to dwell within us to communion with God continually.

As the repairer of the breach and the bridge back over the abyss to our souls, Jesus Christ completed His obedience and faithfulness not to sin. Therefore, He defeated Satan's plan to destroy creation and the plan of redemption.

When I think of restoration I often look at something neglected or needing a loving hand to make it new again or even better than before. Becoming a new creation in Christ brings you to that reality of new life, new beginning, new purpose, new destiny, and new identity in Him.

Being given a second chance to see relationships healed and mended to soar again in unity is what I love to see God do most. Unity restored is the heart of the Father God; division, destruction and death will always be the enemy. The following list reveals what blocks us and keeps us from manifesting God's power and love. You can be free if you want to be.

The 2-5-14 strongholds that will defeat any Christian are the following and can be found in Dr. Henry Malone's book Shadow Boxing.

2 areas of surrendering ground: Intrusion/strategies and Intrusion: Management

5 areas that open doors to the enemy: willful sin/disobedience, unforgiveness, trauma, inner vow and judgments, and word curses/death curses/other curses such as Freemasonry, Vietnam, poverty, lynching, witchcraft, all other.

14 root spirits or strongholds are:

Infirmity: allergies, arthritis, asthma, cancer, diabetes, female problems, fungus, heart disease, high blood pressure, sinus, stroke, viruses

Fear: abandonment, anxiety, faithlessness, fright, inadequacy, inferiority, worry, insanity, -nightmares, performance, phobias, rejection, fear of rejection, self-rejection, shyness, tension/stress, timidity, torment, perfectionism. FEAR of: death, failure, men/women, poverty, success, authority, loss, punishment

Whoredom and Idolatry: adultery/fornication, bestiality, exhibitionism, illegitimacy, incest, lust, molestation, molested as a child, multi-partner orgies, peeping tom, pornography, rape, seduction, compulsive masturbation. Idolatry: money, possessions, position, power, relationships.

Perverseness: false teachers & doctrine, religious spirits, homosexuality, multi-partner orgies, twisted thinking, polygamy, sadomasochism, sexual deviations, gender confusion.

Deaf and Dumb: accidents w/drowning/fire, convulsions, diseases of eyes/ears, epilepsy, grinding of teeth, insanity, seizures, stupor, suicidal thoughts and attempts

Lying: condemnation, deception, exaggeration, feels like hypocrite, lies, profanity, vain imaginations, excessive talking, poverty, poor self-image: you're ugly, stupid, worthless, never marry, No one wants you; you'll never change, fat, whore, bitch, dummy, liar.

Error: anorexia, bulimia, compromise your convictions, confusion, continuously make wrong decisions, cults/false teachers, doubt/unbelief, immaturity, irresponsibility, inappropriate thinking/behavior, religious spirits.

Divination: astrology, channeling, crystal balls/8 balls, fortune tellers, demonic games, horoscopes, rebellion, independence, hypnosis, Pharmacia, Ouija boards, palm readers, Satanism, séances, tarot cards, TM, manipulation, witchcraft, Freemasonry

Bondage: addicted to possessions, alcohol, anorexia, bulimia, cigarettes, co-dependency, work, computers, drugs, good, TV, video games, sex, soul ties, other

Haughtiness: arrogant, boastful, contentious, controlling, critical, dictatorial, domineering, egotistical, proud, gossip, judgment, prejudice, mockery, rudeness, self-righteous, superiority, vanity

Antichrist: blasphemes Holy Spirit and gifts, condemnation of the Word, opposes the Bible, rationalizes the Word, causes church splits, give us on Christianity, harasses & persecute the saints, Judaism, suppresses ministers/ministries, religious spirits.

Heaviness: abnormal grief and mourning, defilement, depression, despair discouragement, hopelessness, loneliness, sadness, self-pity, shame, unjustified guilt (false burdens), wounded spirit (mother/father)

Jealousy: anger, wrath, rage, murder, unnatural competition, covetousness, cruelty, distrustful, divorce/division, feels God loves others more, hatred, jealousy, insecurity, revenge, self-centeredness, suspicion, betrayal

Slumber/sleep: constant fatigue, draw back from life, human spirit asleep, wish you had never been born, passivity, procrastination, success blocked

CHAPTER 11:

Justices: Flipping Injustices

It is good to take note of just how we see God in our hearts. Perhaps our song should be as Mary's as we read in the book of Luke:

Luke 1:46-55:

> *"[46] And Mary said, My soul doth magnify the Lord, [47] and my spirit hath rejoiced in God my Savior.*
>
> *[48] For he hath regarded the low estate of his handmaiden: for, behold, from henceforth all generations shall call me blessed.*
>
> *[49] For he that is mighty hath done to me great things; and holy is his name.*
>
> *[50] And his mercy is on them that fear him from generation to generation.*

51 He hath shewed strength with his arm; he hath scattered the proud in the imagination of their hearts.

52 He hath put down the mighty from their seats, and exalted them of low degree.

53 He hath filled the hungry with good things; and the rich he hath sent empty away.

54 He hath helped his servant Israel, in remembrance of his mercy; 55 as he spoke to our fathers, to Abraham, and to his seed forever."

The heart's cry of men and women who have experienced any kind of loss or abuse is for Jesus and for justice. How the heart does desire for things to be balanced, to be at peace. But the events and circumstances of life do not always lend themselves to balance and peace. They leave us instead torn, broken, confused, and often without much hope of change. Without God, indeed there will be no real change. Our very security rests on the supreme demand for justice and righteousness.

So what do we do? Where do we go? How do we manage to get situations and "things" flipped around or reversed? How do we go about bringing justice into our lives? This is a huge issue to many. The answer often remains hidden from casual view and life goes on for a long time, possibly all of our lives, without ever becoming a reality in our lives. This is not what God planned for any of us. What is the answer?

One path that sometimes is followed with some level of success is found in working through the court system of the land. In some situations this is a necessary part of the journey. However, it is quite possible, if not probable, to come through the legal process and even "win" without experiencing true justice.

The depths of justice and vindication come only through God. There are many scriptures in the Bible that reveal to us the importance God places on justice. In speaking of the Lord the psalmist says:

Psalm 89:14:

> *"Justice and judgment are the habitation of thy throne: mercy and truth shall go before thy face."*

Proverbs 21:3:

> *"To do justice and judgment is more acceptable to the LORD than sacrifice."*

God will indeed restore the years that the locusts have eaten. (See Joel 2:25). How does He accomplish this? What is impossible to man is possible with God. He does it by His divine promises and His mercy.

Our God is so faithful and His Word is true. In the face of injustice and imbalance, we can tend to feel alone and abandoned. We think no one understands our predicament, our pain, our humiliation. But God does see. He does care...more than any person can possibly care. He does know every nook and cranny of your situation.

He has proven this to me many times throughout my walk with Him. In each painful unfair, unjust situation He has never failed to lead me in the process of restoration. He has never failed to show me His great love for me. And He is waiting to do the same for you.

God has raised me up to be a witness of the truth found in Luke 4:18 that He came to set the captives free. It doesn't matter how deep or wide the injustices or bondage in which we find ourselves. Nothing is too hard or too difficult for Him.

God is able to unlock the prison cell we find around us. He holds the key to it. Jesus is the door of hope. When we believe and take hold of the door handle, He is on the other side waiting to receive us and heal the very depths of our pain completely. His plan is always to bring healing and deliverance in order to balance the scales of justice once again. We must choose to ask Him, to see and to knock in order to give Him the freedom to move in our lives. He stands ever ready to come to our aid.

One life situation I can't help but think of when talking about injustices is human trafficking. What a horrendous event in the life of any victim. Not only is the victim affected, but just think of the parents and loved ones. What grief and loss and unfairness, even deep anger, they must all feel. "Why me?" "Why my child?" "Why my sister?" "Why?" For these there is most often no sense of closure. They never learn the whereabouts or the fate of their child. What a terrible and fierce hole this tears in the heart.

There are ministries being raised up today to help deal with these grievous situations. Intercessory prayer groups meet regularly with the purpose of crying out solely for the return of the missing individuals. They pray for the light of God to shine brightly in the darkness and find the lost ones, for human trafficking is no longer a random event, but a huge and growing cancer on the global society. It touches all our communities, no matter where we live. Some are answering the call and committing their lives to help bring life back to a dead soul traumatized by the horror of the experience. Praise God for those who respond to God's call in these matters. We must join these faithful in the call for these survivors to be brought back to life through the resurrection power of Christ. This is hope; this is love.

While there is no question that human trafficking is a tremendous issue in our world today, there are countless other lesser...and far greater... means for the enemy to bring injustices into our daily lives. A false accusation, myriad of abuses, and so many more scenarios of inequality and unfairness are present to hit us and try to take us out.

We must always remember what John 10:10 tells us about the devil: his purpose is only to steal, kill, and destroy. That is the ultimate purpose of injustice. How desperately he wants to hit us hard enough that we give up on our walk with God, turn our backs and walk away into loss, death, and oblivion.

Psalm 94:1:

> *"O LORD God, to whom vengeance belongs; O God, to whom vengeance belongs, shew thyself."*

This verse tells us that vengeance – the setting right of injustices – belongs to God. It is not up to us. We are to look to Him to make right all that has been knocked off balance in our life's experiences. That is part of what He does when we make Him Lord of our lives.

What does it take to bring justice, to flip injustices into balance and peace? Jesus. We know that Jesus came to establish justice and to fulfill the prophecies of His coming. He was of the lineage of King David. A look into David's life gives us a valuable perspective on the subject.

David sought the Lord for justice while standing in the midst of his enemies many times. He even recorded his prayers in the psalms he wrote. Psalms 89 and 110 are two of his best, I think.

Psalm 89:

> "1 *I will sing of the mercies of the Lord forever: with my mouth will I make known thy faithfulness to all generations.*
>
> 2 *For I have said, Mercy shall be built up for ever: thy faithfulness shalt thou establish in the very heavens.*
>
> 3 *I have made a covenant with my chosen, I have sworn*
> *unto David my servant,*
> 4 *thy seed will I establish for-*
> *ever, and build up thy throne to all generations. Selah.*
>
> 8 *O Lord God of hosts, who is a strong Lord like unto thee? or to thy faithfulness round about thee?*
>
> 13 *Thou hast a mighty arm: strong is thy hand, and high is thy right hand.*
>
> 14 *Justice and judgment are the habitation of thy throne: mercy and truth shall go before thy face."*

David's words clearly reveal to us his own feelings and his unwavering faith in his God to right the wrongs around him. And it shows us God's attitude and His action plan for His dealing with injustices.

The secret of David's success, even in the face of a nine-foot giant, was to seek the Lord for the answers. His intimate relationship with God and God's subsequent answers with strategies on how to defeat the enemy are profound. He never did the same thing twice. David never assumed that, since God told him to go out to war one way one time, that it was a model for the next battle. No. It was just the opposite. He sought the God for wisdom, knowledge, strength, and insight. He chose to love God with his whole heart. That relationship moved God's heart to forgive David's failures and to show him the way to success and ultimate justice.

We should do the same. It is that simple. Go to God for a "God plan." Find out what God's heart is in the matter facing you. Fasting is a good way to break the hold of the strongman, binding the situation, and crying out for breakthrough. Praying is another powerful weapon that brings hope and strength to endure along with the revelation of God's plan.

Several years ago, pastors were being killed by the drug cartel in Central America. The pastors that remained decided to unite and pray seeking God for strategy on how to survive the onslaught of violence and turn the tide of injustice to one of justice. As they united to pray the heard of a man who God had trained to defeat the enemy so they contacted him and he came to pray them through to get a breakthrough. This is justice. This is our God. He loves us and wants us to exercise the God-given authority and power to think Kingdom as He gives back what was stolen seven fold according to Proverbs.

CHAPTER 12:

Jesus Honors Us by Blessing Us

What is it you want from life? Don't think in terms of what you may need, but rather, think about what you want from life itself. It's an interesting exercise. As people we so easily fall into the patterns of education, marriage, children, home, and family. There is, of course, nothing wrong with any of these things and God has blessed so many men and women down through the ages, and continues to bless us today in those pursuits. But, after we have given all we can give to others in these areas, there is still something deeper within. What is it at the very core of your being that cried out to be fulfilled? What is your present day passion?

Jesus accomplished so much for all in His coming, but for believers He truly changed so much. He brought the women to the forefront of social life. He met them in all strata of life from poor to rich, grieving, married, single, prostitutes, healthy, sick. He exhorted and encouraged them to sit at His feet, to learn from Him, to hear His wisdom for life. His teachings were practical and spoke to the day-to-day lives they lived. Many followed Him faithfully; some closest to Him followed clear to the cross that day He gave His life for us all. They were the first to discover His resurrection.

Matthew 28:1-10:

> *"In the end of the Sabbath, as it began to dawn toward the first day of the week, came Mary Magdalene and the other Mary to see the sepulchre. [2] And, behold, there was a great earthquake: for the angel of the Lord descended from heaven, and came and rolled back the stone from the door, and sat upon it. [3] His countenance was like lightning, and his raiment white as snow: [4] and for fear of him the keepers did shake, and became as dead men. [5] And the angel answered and said unto the women, Fear not ye: for I know that ye seek Jesus, which was crucified. [6] He is not here: for he is risen, as he said. Come, see the place where the Lord lay. [7] And go quickly, and tell his disciples that he is risen from the dead; and, behold, he goes before you into Galilee; there shall ye see him: lo, I have told you. [8] And they departed quickly from the sepulcher with fear and great joy; and did run to bring his disciples word. [9] And as they went to tell his disciples, behold, Jesus met them, saying, All hail. And they came and held him by the feet, and worshiped him. [10] Then said Jesus unto them, Be not afraid: go tell my brethren that they go into Galilee, and there shall they see me."*

I think it is so interesting that it wasn't any of the disciples who met the angel at the tomb, but the two women. What an important task they were given to go tell the disciples the news.

There is another woman spoken of in the John's gospel who had a special encounter with Jesus. You can read the account in John 4:5-42.

This is the woman who went back to her Samaritan people and testified of Jesus. A woman evangelist was born at that moment.

John 4:25-30:

> *"[1] In the end of the Sabbath, as it began to dawn toward the first day of the week, came Mary Magdalene and the other Mary to see the sepulcher. [2] And, behold, there was a great earthquake: for the angel of the Lord descended from heaven, and came and rolled back the stone from the door, and sat upon it. [3] His countenance was like lightning, and his raiment white as snow: [4] and for fear of him the keepers did shake, and became as dead men. [5] And the angel answered and said unto the women, Fear not ye: for I know that ye seek Jesus, which was crucified. [6] He is not here: for he is risen, as he said. Come; see the place where the Lord lay. [7] And go quickly, and tell his disciples that he is risen from the dead; and, behold, he goes before you into Galilee; there shall ye see him: lo, I have told you. 8 And they departed quickly from the sepulcher with fear and great joy; and did run to bring his disciples word. [9] And as they went to tell his disciples, behold, Jesus met them, saying, All hail. And they came and held him by the feet, and worshipped him. [10] Then said Jesus unto them, Be not afraid: go tell my brethren that they go into Galilee, and there shall they see me."*

The verses following these tell of all the Samaritan people who, on her testimony, went to hear Jesus and many believed on Him. Can you see how God touched a woman standing by a well in her ordinary day, revealing the Christ to her, and how she shared her testimony and many more were changed, too? She went from a simple drink of water to evangelizing her community.

After the Ascension of Jesus, the disciples gathered in the upper room as they were directed to do. Acts 1:12-14 tells us of the gathering of people that day:

> *"12 Then returned they unto Jerusalem from the mount called Olivet, which is from Jerusalem a Sabbath day's journey. 13 And when they were come in, they went up into an upper room, where abode both Peter, and James, and John, and Andrew, Philip, and Thomas, Bartholomew, and Matthew, James the son of Alphœus, and Simon Zelotes, and Judas the brother of James. 14 These all continued with one accord in prayer and supplication, with the women, and Mary the mother of Jesus, and with his brethren."*

Notice in the fourteenth verse that they met with the women and Mary, Jesus' mother. Can you imagine what it must have been like to be in Mary's shoes? All through Jesus' life, Mary knew who He was. She remembered the angel coming to her. She knew in her heart all through His life. In Luke's account of the angel coming to Mary with the message that began with, "Fear not, Mary: for you have found favor with God." In Luke 1:47-48 we hear Mary's rich words of obedience and acceptance:

> *"47 And my spirit has rejoiced in God my Savior. 48 For he hath regarded the low estate of his handmaiden: for, behold, from henceforth all generations shall call me blessed."*

And indeed, Mary has been called "blessed" forever after. How tenderly and lovingly the Holy Spirit and the angel that day ministered to her. What an honor it is to serve our living God.

And then that day in the upper room, here were Mary and the other women once again, this time waiting for the Holy Spirit. Acts 2:1-4 tells us what took place when the Holy Spirit came.

"And when the day of Pentecost was fully come, they were all with one accord in one place. [2] And suddenly there came a sound from heaven as of a rushing mighty wind, and it filled the entire house where they were sitting. [3] And there appeared unto them cloven tongues like as of fire, and it sat upon each of them. 4 And they were all filled with the Holy Ghost, and began to speak with other tongues, as the Spirit gave them utterance."

The Holy Spirit fell on everyone in the room, men and women alike, and they all were filled and began to speak with other tongues.

There was the woman with the issue of blood that was healed. Jesus was on His way to Jairus' house to heal her little girl, but this woman pressed through the crowd of people around Him. Read her story in Luke 8:41-48.

"[41] And, behold, there came a man named Jairus, and he was a ruler of the synagogue: and he fell down at Jesus' feet, and besought him that he would come into his house: [42] for he had one only daughter, about twelve years of age, and she lay a dying. But as he went the people thronged him. [43] And a woman having an issue of blood twelve years, which had spent all her living upon physicians, neither could be healed of any, [44] came behind him, and touched the border of his garment: and immediately her issue of blood stanched. [45] And Jesus said who touched me?" When all denied, Peter and they that were with him said, Master, the multitude throng thee and press thee, and says thou, who touched me? [46] And Jesus said, somebody hath touched me: for I perceive that virtue is gone out of me. [47] And when the woman saw that she was not hid, she came trembling, and falling down before him, she

declared unto him before all the people for what cause she had touched him, and how she was healed immediately. [48] And he said unto her, Daughter, be of good comfort: thy faith hath made the whole; go in peace."

This little woman was not only sick, but broke, too, for she had spent all her money with the doctors and was no better, but worse. And with an issue of blood she was considered unclean as well. But she had heard of this Jesus and believed in her heart that if she could just touch the bottom of His clothes she would be healed. So pulled together all her courage and faith to step out and when she touched Him, she was healed. And she and Jesus both knew it. What an encounter for her! Her life suddenly was changed and put back together in an instant of faith released.

Throughout the Word of God there are so many women and men honored in so many ways. Deborah as one of the judges over Israel sat and gave them clear advice in very difficult times. That is amazing to me. She had discernment for she was righteous. The fourth chapter of the book of Judges tells about her. It is an awesome story of a woman mightily touched and used of God. Solomon was the wisest King that ever lived and God blessed him with great wealth and abundance. His wisdom graced many that came to his court for decisions.

Today it is easy for us as women to become confused, depressed and even desperate in trying to find our way in life. There are so many things that can crowd in on us and cloud our vision. It is important to be balanced spiritually, emotionally, physically and mentally. To discover the rhythm of life is wholeness. We must focus on honoring ourselves and our Lord.

The inner person of the heart truly reflects what manner of person we are. Character is the fruit of a balanced life. We can give our whole life to pursuing a passion, but will others follow our example? Great artists and other successful people may reach a goal in life, but sometimes they do it at the price of leaving the rest of their lives in ruin. They may achieve greatness in art, for example, but have led a sexually immoral life, leaving many relationships painfully behind.

Think of Mary again. She was chosen by God. The scriptures say that all nations will call her blessed. What an honor. She was visited by the angel and said yes to God's plan for her life. She was available and willing to do what God had asked of her. Mary had a rhythm to her life that pleased God. See where you find yourself in this list of qualities Mary and others exhibited.

1. **Knowledge of yourself. Mary was a Hebrew, a Nazarene virgin girl. There was humility and a quality in her God chose to use. He trusted her with His Son. What is it about yourself that you love and believe in? Do you know what gift God gave you to pursue? Do you have a desire to feed the hungry, pray for the nation, be a corporate executive, be the best you can be at gourmet cooking, hairdressing, landscaping, etc.?**
2. **Ability to see past your limitations. Do you find yourself dreaming like the great people throughout history of great adventures or discoveries? They did not allow limitation to stop them. God has no limits and He lives within you. He desires for you to be all you can be. Do not hold back. Go for that dream.**
3. **Vision. What is your vision for life? Vision for what you want to accomplish needs to be written down. Then you must believe it by making plans to get there. Habakkuk gave us this advice. (Read Habakkuk 2:2-3.) Proverbs 29:18 states that where there is no vision the people perish.**
4. **Quiet within. Your life is there for the living; reach and grab hold of it. Mother Theresa chose the poorest of the poor. She discovered solitude, silence, and service as keys to success. She said that the fruit of silence is prayer; the fruit of prayer is faith; the fruit of faith is love; the fruit of love is service; and the fruit of service is peace. Therefore, peace begins with silence.**
5. **Free to be yourself. A thought you may be pondering today is what will it take for me to be a better woman that I was yesterday? Your thoughts, positive and negative alike, determine your course of action for the day as well as for the rest of your life. Imagination takes you to a new place**

of creative thinking outside your own box. Reach up and out of the box to see the horizon of something great yet to be realized by your decisions today. Break out of the mold and discover the real you.

6. Dedication. Dedicate yourself to be the best version of yourself, whatever that might be. In order to love what you do you must do what you love. Everything has meaning when you have purpose. Take the dare and step out by faith to explore the possibilities before you. There are so many opportunities to be the real you. Pursue excellence in all you do, whether it is homemaking or designing or marketing or communicating.
7. Have faith. Believe by faith that God wants to honor you in every gift, talent and ability you have. Without faith it is impossible to please Him. He loves you more than you will ever know. Believe in your destiny and rejoice in the discovery of doing the impossible with God. Many are bound by fear and it restrains them to never venture out to discover like a child the awesomeness and wonder of life.
8. Have good and strong relationships. People need relationships and deserve to be cherished. Life is full of relationships and we must choose to accept them and ourselves by embracing those inner treasures. Acceptance is the key. If you pre-judge a relationship through rejection you will never the joy of relating. Rejection is a major stumbling block for people, especially for women. Don't believe the lies about yourself. Press forward and be a blessing to others that God has put into your life.
9. Communication. This is an art form for most women. They love to talk and visit with each other. The art of communicating is listening to the other person's heart. Stay on topic in a discussion and stay with the facts to have a positive exchange of words.
10. Hold to hope and dreams. Never give up on your hopes and dreams. Be as Apostle Paul who said in Philippians 3:14, "I press toward the mark for the prize of the high calling of God in Christ Jesus." Paul had every reason to

be discouraged and focus on his failures, but God used him—even in prison—to write so many of the New Testament letters that guide the church today. Perseverance is a much admired character trait. It is a true virtue. Women throughout history have done just that.

CHAPTER 13:

Power of the Gospel

There is so much to be said of the gospel of Jesus Christ, the gospel of the Kingdom. Its value and worth are beyond measure. The good news, Paul said of it,

> *"For I am not ashamed of the gospel of Christ: for it is the power of God unto salvation to everyone that believes; to the Jew first, and also to the Greek." – Romans 1:16*

The gospel is the power of God. We have only to read through the Gospels – the books of Matthew, Mark, Luke, and John – to find the power of God working in the ministry of Jesus. Over and over we read where Jesus preached or taught, then healed ALL their diseases moved by compassion.. We see Him raise the dead, set people free from demonic strongholds. Whatever the problem, the gospel – the Good News – was more than enough to meet the need.

The Word of God is not just mere words, but life-giving power. To have words without power and think they are from God is just empty religion. Religion is an evil spirit robbing precious people of Truth, stripping away the very power of God.

I believe the decree for this hour, for this time, is for a shift to new beginnings, new seasons, a time of new doors opening for wonders and signs, a time to watch the multiplication of souls into the Kingdom. We must expect God to show up in our world, in our lives, and bring global harvest. In His love we must declare, "Holy Spirit, move freely in power and truth upon us. We seek after Your freedom to move in power and might."

The Apostle Paul was not afraid to demonstrate the power of the Kingdom gospel, especially in 1 Corinthians. He emphasizes that it is not his education or persuasive speech, but the resurrection power of God. Christianity is the only religion that centers on a living God – One Who rose from the dead and sits on the right hand of God, the Father. He is our Mediator. The same dunamis power (power equivalent to dynamite) is in us today through the indwelling presence of the Holy Spirit. It is up to us to believe that this same power is in us to raise the dead, heal the sick, and cast out devils. This power must be released by faith so that others might believe and be saved.

Acts 1:8:

> *"But ye shall receive power, after that the Holy Ghost is come upon you: and ye shall be witnesses unto me both in Jerusalem, and in all Judaea, and in Samaria, and unto the uttermost part of the earth."*

1 Corinthians 1:18:

> *"For the preaching of the cross is to them that perish foolishness; but unto us which are saved it is the power of God."*

1 Corinthians 2:4-5:

> *"4 And my speech and my preaching was not with enticing words of man's wisdom, but in demonstration*

of the Spirit and of power: [5] that your faith should not stand in the wisdom of men, but in the power of God."

1 Corinthians 4:20:

"For the kingdom of God is not in word, but in power."

1 Thessalonians 1:4-5:

"[4] Knowing, brethren beloved, your election of God. [5] For our gospel came not unto you in word only, but also in power, and in the Holy Ghost, and in much assurance; as ye know what manner of men we were among you for your sake."

We are to rule by the revelation of the Holy Spirit. Ask God for the unction to function like Paul did and to become one in Covenant and Kingdom reality. Paul went to Mars Hill in Athens where the great intellectual minds of the day gathered to reason and discuss philosophies. He had courage and he knew his God. He was not afraid to tell them that their statue to honor the "Unknown God" represented the One True God he served and that God dwelt within him with power and might.

The power of God manifests at healing when needed. It was and is present to heal all – that is a key emphasis when it comes to healing.

Isaiah 53:5:

"But he was wounded for our transgressions; he was bruised for our iniquities: the chastisement of our peace was upon him; and with his stripes we are healed."

Matthew 4:23:

"And Jesus went about all Galilee, teaching in their synagogues, and preaching the gospel of the kingdom, and healing all manner of sickness and all manner of disease among the people."

Matthew 9:35:

"And Jesus went about all the cities and villages, teaching in their synagogues, and preaching the gospel of the kingdom, and healing every sickness and every disease among the people."

Matthew 12:15:

"...But when Jesus knew it, he withdrew himself from thence: and great multitudes followed him, and he healed them all;"

Matthew 8:16-17:

"16 When the even was come, they brought unto him many that were possessed with devils: and he cast out the spirits with his word, and healed all that were sick: 17 that it might be fulfilled which was spoken by Esaias the prophet, saying, Himself took our infirmities, and bare our sicknesses."

The miracles we see take place in the gospels and all through the New Testament are not restricted to a very few ministers. Jesus sent out many people. He believed in multiplication. We hear Jesus speak these words, not just to the people in that day, but to us in this time as well:

Mark 16:17-18:

> *"17 And these signs shall follow them that believe; in my name shall they cast out devils; they shall speak with new tongues; 18 they shall take up serpents; and if they drink any deadly thing, it shall not hurt them; they shall lay hands on the sick, and they shall recover."*

What an amazing promise. What a powerful God. What a powerful Word. And we are free to walk in this powerful promise.

Matthew 10:7-8:

> *"7 And as ye go, preach, saying, the kingdom of heaven is at hand. 8 Heal the sick, cleanse the lepers, and raise the dead, cast out devils: freely ye have received, freely give."*

Jesus has given us power over evil spirits in His Name. So many need to be set free. We are in denial if we think we have arrived. We must break through the walls in our lives. It is a choice we must make to forgive and let go! It is time to accelerate our destiny by decreeing and forgiving.

Luke 10:19-20:

> *"19 Behold, I give unto you power to tread on serpents and scorpions, and over all the power of the enemy: and nothing shall by any means hurt you. 20 notwithstanding in this rejoice not, that the spirits are subject unto you; but rather rejoice, because your names are written in heaven."*

The gospel of Jesus also includes the power to get wealth. In this end time when we are so close to the return of Jesus He has supplied Kingdom economics – supernatural provision – for the unprecedented harvest we are to bring in to Him.

Deuteronomy 1:11 says,

> *"May the LORD, the God of your fathers, increase you a thousand times and bless you as he has promised!"*

Deuteronomy 8:18:

> *"But thou shalt remember the Lord thy God: for it is he that giveth thee power to get wealth that he may establish his covenant which he swore unto thy fathers, as it is this day."*

We must open our hearts to receive instruction from the Lord, guidance in financial matters. There is great provision in place for the work of the gospel. It is exciting to become a part of the plan of God.

There is so much to be added to our lives by the power of holiness. How do we come into the power of a holy life?

Repent. We must return to the Most High God while there is yet time; repent of sins and believe Jesus. (See John 3:3, 16)

Receive the Holy Spirit.

1. **Clean your house. We must be earnest to purge ourselves of sin, both the open obvious sin and the hidden secret ones. Holiness is about living our lives separated unto God. Read Exodus chapter 20 and Romans 1 to see what God thinks about sin. We must choose toward God, not away from Him toward sin and disobedience.**
2. **Forgive. Read Matthew 5:23-25 and Matthew 6:14-16. These passages teach us the importance of forgiveness. Refusing to forgive hurts only ourselves, holding us in bondage and hindering the work of the Holy Spirit in our own**

lives. I must confess that I had to watch the movie, The Passion of Christ, three times before I really understood and caught the revelation, the heart of God when Jesus said, and "Forgive them for they know not what they do." We are called to forgive—7 x 70 or 490 times—every day if we have to for every offense, betrayal, judgment, injustice, shame, bullying, etc., that ever comes our way. We must make our decree: "I forgive and I let go of everything that has warred against me that has stood between me and my destiny!" Repeat this again and again in faith until you are released and accelerating onward to your supernatural time with God.

3. Pursue holiness. Hebrews 12:14 tells us to pursue peace with all people—peace and holiness. Why? What is the outcome God desires for us? The same passage tells us that without them, no one will see the Lord. Our God is holy and we are called to be holy just as He is.

4. Be humble. 1 Peter 4:5-7 admonishes us to "be clothed with humility: for God resists the proud, and gives grace to the humble. Humble yourselves therefore under the mighty hand of God, that he may exalt you in due time." How do we humble ourselves? These verses tell us that humility comes with casting all of our cares upon Jesus. We stop being the God of our own lives and let Jesus care for us. Read James 4:6-7 to see that God resists those who walk in pride. He actually resists them. But He gives grace—empowerment and ability—to the humble.

5. Have faith. In Hebrews 11:1 we are told that "Now faith is the substance of things hoped for, the evidence of things not seen. And further in verse 6 we see that without faith it is impossible for us to please God. We must believe that He is, and that He is the rewarder of those who diligently seek after Him.

6. Walk in love. It would be so good for us to study and meditate 1 Corinthians 13—the love chapter—daily. God's love is so amazing. His love is so divine; but love rejected, love turned aside, does not negate His love for us. His love re-

mains waiting for a response from those who has denied His love's existence. Love is God's hope toward us who believe and trust that He loves us, that we are created for His own pleasure and glory. To those of us who will receive, His healing waters are flowing, revealing His great grace toward us. He tells us to come boldly to the throne of grace.

I challenge you to ask God for that one person that you could express love to so that they might come to believe in God. The world is waiting for the church – the living stones – to awake, to arise and choose to love others and show them kindness and mercy. Peoples' hearts cry out secretly, "Does anyone really believe? Is God's love real?"

Here is a God-given example of how His ways are different than our ways, even when it comes to saving souls, i.e., saving the centurion at the crucifixion by the very breath of God.

Mark 15:38-39:

"38 And the veil of the temple was rent in twain from the top to the bottom. 39 And when the centurion, whom stood over against him, saw that he so cried out, and gave up the ghost, he said, truly this man was the Son of God."

The centurion was a Roman military leader who had killed Christians for his government leadership. He was hardened, disassociated, in control of his emotions. Yet he was intelligent, questioning the verdict to crucify Christ. He stood looking at Jesus, the King of the Jews, and at that very moment Jesus breathed out His last breath over the centurion below Him. It opened the hardened man's eyes and ears, giving him the revelation so he could make the declaration of belief that truly, this Man was the Son of God. I believe that Christ saved the centurion's soul at that very moment of his declaration of belief.

Isaiah 40:31:

> *"But they that wait upon the Lord shall renew their strength; they shall mount up with wings as eagles; they shall run, and not be weary; and they shall walk, and not faint."*

Would you like to experience new strength and the very breath of God blowing on you to empower you and revive you? Be aligned with Him to soar above adversity. Live from strength to strength in His presence. Receive fresh boldness and courage. Receive a fresh oil and fire on your gifting. Live in daily communion with the Creator. See creative miracles as you are holy and preach the true Kingdom gospel.

See rushing streams of breakthrough in your finances, in your health, welfare, relationships, and ministry. The Word tells us that those who know their God shall be strong and do great exploits. In this very moment, right now, you are here for such a time as this. God has blessed you with finances to sow into the global harvest. In the sense of time as the Lord looks through His eye of time, He knew this present time. By His design you are alive for such a time as this in history.

Ephesians 1:17-21:

> *"[17] That the God of our Lord Jesus Christ, the Father of glory, may give unto you the spirit of wisdom and revelation in the knowledge of him: [18] the eyes of your understanding being enlightened; that ye may know what is the hope of his calling, and what the riches of the glory of his inheritance in the saints, [19] and what is the exceeding greatness of his power to us-ward who believe, according to the working of his mighty power, [20] which he wrought in Christ, when he raised him from the dead, and set him at his own right hand in the heavenly places, [21] far above all principality, and power, and might, and dominion, and every name that*

is named, not only in this world, but also in that which is to come:"

CHAPTER 14:

The Holy Spirit is Our Helper & Comforter

The Holy Spirit is referred to in the Word of God by at least 25 different names. Each of these names represents a facet of His work. For example, the Intercessor is a name which represents a character trait. It is the Holy Spirit who prompts us to pray and who teaches us how to pray and prays through us.

> *"Likewise the Spirit also helped our infirmities: for we know not what we should pray for as we ought: but the Spirit itself makes intercession for us with groaning's which cannot be uttered." – Romans 8:26*

We must learn to lean on the Holy Spirit and trust Him to help us with everything. He is called the Helper because His ministry is to help us. Another of His names is the Strengthener because He strengthens us in our time of need. He is known as the Comforter because of the peace and comfort He alone can minister to our inner man (where comfort and refreshing is as often needed as we live our lives here on earth).

The Holy Spirit is also referred to as wind, fire, rain, oil and wine. On the day of Pentecost He came as a rushing mighty wind into the room, sat as tongues of fire upon each of the 120 believers who waited in the upper room, and filled them with His presence. Those present were never the same after that day.

Maybe you need a fresh wind from God. Or maybe you need to experience that fresh fire of the Holy Spirit. You might be feeling stale and moldy as a Christian, or maybe even "dead." There's hope for you.

Paul told Timothy to fan the flame within him:

> *"For this reason I remind you to fan into flame the gift of God, which is in you through the laying on of my hands. " – 2 Timothy 1:6*

Ask for the wind of the Spirit to blow on whatever sparks are left and let him do in you what He desires to do.

One main reason why people do not experience the fullness of God in their lives is because they want to be the boss over everything in their lives. But in order to step into that fullness, the Holy Spirit must be allowed to be in charge. He knows God's plan for your life. He knows the mind of God for you in each and every situation. Let Him lead you and learn to follow whatever He tells you to do.

You yourself must pray for a mighty wind to blow in your life. Invite the fire of God. Ask for rain to water your life. Ask God to pour in the oil and the new wine. Let the Lord show you new ways to approach old problems. Ask Him to reveal to you the things you are doing that are making life hard.

It is God's will that you have righteousness and joy in the Holy Spirit. The fire of God comes into our lives to ignite us, but it also comes as a refiner's fire to burn up everything that is not consistent with His nature. Hebrews 12:20 tells us that:

> *"...Our God is a consuming fire."*

The Holy Spirit relentlessly pursues the things in use that prevent the Father's will from coming into full manifestation. In His love and perfect timing, He seeks to deliver us. Our following of His leading in these things brings us into more and deeper holiness in Him.

In order to have a harvest of manifested holiness in our lives, we need the Word of God which is often referred to as seed. (See Mark 4) And we need the Holy Spirit, sometimes referred to as rain, to water that seed. Pray for the rain of the Holy Spirit in your life. Ask for an outpouring. You cannot by your own strength change the things in your life that need to be changed. But the Holy Spirit can and He will if you learn to lean on Him and not on the arm of the flesh.

What about the oil and new wine? In Zechariah 4:6 we read: Not by might, nor by power, but by my spirit, says the Lord of hosts. This is a ceaseless supply of oil coming to us from God that means that we do not have to struggle with things. We as believers simply need to be sure our lives are well-oiled. This happens when we spend time in His presence waiting on Him, loving Him and meditating in His word. As we look to him and trust Him instead of ourselves, we will experience an ease in our life that is available at all times.

The Holy Spirit is also known as the oil of gladness. When we are suffering needlessly or struggling in a difficult place, remember that God is there. He cares. He knows about us. It is time to trust and obey and pray.

The Word of God has much to say about breath. One key is that breath is the Holy Spirit's power called dunamis in the Greek of the New Testament. This is creation power, resurrection power! Take in these scriptures that talk about breath:

John 3:7:

"Marvel not that I said unto thee, ye must be born again."

Job 27:3:

"And the spirit of God is in my nostrils;"

Ecclesiastes 11:5:

"As thou knows not what is the way of the spirit, or how the bones do grow in the womb of her that is with child: even so thou knows not the works of God who makes all."

Let the Holy Spirit move and God will speak. We see this principle in these scriptures:

Genesis 1:2-3:

"And the earth was without form, and void; and darkness was upon the face of the deep. And the Spirit of God moved upon the face of the waters. 3 And God said, Let there be light: and there was light."

Job 26:13:

"By his spirit he hath garnished the heavens; his hand hath formed the crooked serpent."

Psalm 104:30:

"Thou send forth thy spirit, they are created: And thou renews the face of the earth."

Psalm 33:6:

"Ask the Holy Spirit to come and take control, to let the rain and wind of heaven fall on my soul."

Job 33:4:

"The Spirit of God hath made me, and the breath of the Almighty hath given me life."

Job 27:3:

"And the spirit of God is in my nostrils;"

John 6:63-64:

"[63] It is the spirit that quickened; the flesh profited nothing: the words that I speak unto you, they are spirit, and they are life. [64] But there are some of you that believe not. For Jesus knew from the beginning that they were that believed not, and who should betray him."

Romans 8:11:

"But if the Spirit of him that raised up Jesus from the dead dwell in you, he that rose up Christ from the dead shall also quicken your mortal bodies by his Spirit that dwelled in you."

Who is He?

He is God, the third person of the Trinity, co-equal with God the Father and with God the Son. He is mightily at work in and through us. Here's a list of some of the workings of the Holy Spirit:

- **He convicts us of sin and righteousness and judgment (John 16:8-11).**
- **It is through Him that we experience the new birth (John 3:6).**
- **He indwells every believer (1 Corinthians 6:19-20).**
- **He baptizes all believers into the body of Christ (1 Corinthians 12:13)**
- **He seals every believer (Ephesians 1:13-14; 4:30).**
- **He fills the obedient and yielded believer (Ephesians 5:18).**
- **He guides us into all truth (John 16:12-13).**
- **He empowers us for service (Acts 1:8).**
- **He enables us to walk in the Spirit (Galatians 5:16).**

The Indwelling of the Holy Spirit

We are to understand that every believer has within him the Holy Spirit – all of the Holy Spirit within us that we will ever have. There is no way in which we may receive more of the Holy Spirit, nor can we lose any part of Him. Read and study the following scriptures to understand these truths about his relationship with us:

- **Romans 8:9**
- **2 Corinthians 6:16**
- **2 Timothy 1:14**
- **1 John 2:27**
- **1 John 3:24**
- **1 John 4:12-13**

The Holy Spirit does not indwell us just so He can have a place to stay, nor does He dwell within us just for our personal gratification or to serve our own purposes. Rather, He indwells us in order to change us into the likeness of Christ, to produce works which are pleasing to God, to witness to others of the reality of Christ and lead them into salvation. The moment a penitent sinner puts faith in Christ as Savior he enters into "life in Christ" and the Holy Spirit makes it happen. This is the most dynamic and amazing work of all for to be "in Christ" is to be where He is, to be what He is, and to share all that He has.

Baptism of the Holy Ghost

The baptism by the Spirit (in the Greek language of the New Testament) the preposition in can be accurately interpreted as with, in, or by. John the Baptist foretold of this baptism in Matthew 3:11, Mark 1:8, Luke 3:16, John 1:33. In Acts 1:3, 8 Jesus Himself told His disciples. Later, in Acts 2:14-22 we find Peter telling the crowd that on that very day (the Day of Pentecost) the promise of the Holy Spirit was fulfilled in that upper room. The baptism by the Spirit makes us members of the body of Christ (See 1 Corinthians 12:13, Romans 6:2-5, Ephesians 4:5, and Colossians 2:13).

The baptism by the Spirit is for this age only (the church age) and is universal among all believers. There is no reference to the baptism by the Spirit in the Old Testament. It is distinctive to this church age. In addition, we find that everyone who receives Jesus Christ as Savior experiences the baptism by the Spirit as 1 Corinthians 12:13 indicate. When we are saved we are immersed into Jesus; we are "in Christ."

This baptism is a divine promise. "The promise of the Father" always refers to the baptism of the Holy Spirit. We find these references in Jeremiah 31:32-35, Ezekiel 36:26-27, and Joel 2:28-32. It came to us after Jesus was glorified (John 7:37-39; 16:7).

The baptism of the Holy Spirit was at a set time: on the day of Pentecost when the Jews were celebrating the festival of Pentecost. (This is prophetic of the coming of the Holy Spirit who made Jew and Gentile into one body. Read Ephesians 2:11-12; 3:4-6.) The Spirit is put within man in the new covenant whereas, under the old covenant, He came upon man to empower him for a certain service.

Filling of the Holy Spirit

The verb filled in Ephesians 5:18 is pleroo and it means to be made full (in a passive voice.) Filled is in the present tense in the Greek and it means to continually and habitually be filled. It is in the imperative mood which signifies that it is a command or an order to be obeyed. The voice of the verb is passive which means that the subject receives or is acted upon by the verb.

Now, what can we learn from of this that will be practical and valuable to our lives? The filling of the Spirit is a command that we are to obey, therefore, it is not something that happens automatically. However, the filling is there for the taking to any who is a born-again child of God. We have only to yield. This is indicated by the passive voice – filling happens to the subject.

Beloved, if you are a Christian, you have the Holy Spirit (see John 14:16-17, Romans 8:9, 1 Corinthians 6:19-20). And if God's Spirit is within you, then it is His desire to fill you to the full. This filling is to be continuous filling, something constantly taking place. Thus Paul's command in 1 Thessalonians 5:19 "Do not quench the Spirit." To quench is to stop or to hinder the Holy Spirit, to fail to let Him do that which He desires to do. Philippians 2:13 tells us that "it is God that works in you both to will and to do His good pleasure." We see God's work. However, it is our responsibility to work out (to keep carrying out) our salvation with fear and trembling. In other words, God gives us the desire and does the work, but we must let Him. We must allow Him to fill us to the full. When He does, what will others see? Christlikeness. This is what it means to be filled with the Holy Spirit.

Fullness of the Spirit

What does the fullness of the Spirit look like on a believer? Sometimes it helps us understand if we identify some things that it is not. For example, the fullness of the Spirit is not about receiving more of the Spirit. Fullness is not speaking in tongues or having a sensational or emotional experience. It is not a super-deluxe higher-form of the Christian life that only a few may achieve.

The fullness of the Holy Spirit is the normal Christian life. It is our allowing the Spirit to completely take over our lives. We surrender ourselves to come under the Lordship of Christ and under the control of the Holy Spirit. Fullness of the Spirit is a walk of daily submission, a dependence upon the Lord Jesus Christ.

How to be filled with the Holy Spirit

First of all, we are filled with the Spirit by faith in the same way we become a Christian by faith (Ephesians 2:8-9). We also walk in the Spirit by faith (Colossians 2:6) We do not have to beg God for what already belongs to us in Christ (Romans 1:17).

Several factors contribute to our heart's preparation for being filled by faith. We must desire to live a life that will please the Lord (Matthew 5:6). We must be willing to surrender the absolute unqualified control of our lives to Christ. We must be open for Him to do His will instead of our own. This is according to the command of God (Romans 12:1-2). We must also expose, judge, and confess any sin which the Holy Spirit calls to our remembrance (1 John 1:9). If necessary, make restitution when appropriate. Claim the forgiveness of our Lord.

There are two truths to remember in claiming His filling by faith. The first is that He has commanded us to be filled (Ephesians 5:18). The second is that His promise is to always answer when we pray according to His will (1 John 3:14-15). These are keys. It is also helpful to keep in mind that the Holy Spirit indwells already any born-again Christian.

Being filled with the Holy Spirit is not a once-and-for-all experience. We are to be constantly filled with the Holy Spirit. It must become a way of life. Neither is it simply by prayer that we are filled; it is by faith. It is also true that we can never make ourselves good enough to please God; rather, we must live by faith (Romans 6:7, Jeremiah 17:9, Galatians 2:20).

The product or result of being filled and of walking in the Spirit is that we become dead to self and alive to God (Matthew 6:24, John 12:24). We live by faith. Feelings are valid as a by-product of faith and obedience, but at no time should we depend upon feelings alone. We must walk in faith.

Walking in the Spirit

Every believer has two natures residing within – the fleshly and the spiritual. The flesh wants to satisfy every demand of self. It is bent on the gratification and glorification of self. It cannot know, obey, or please God. By contrast, the spiritual wants to please Christ. It is bent on the gratification and glorification of Christ. It can and does know, obey, and please God.

These two natures are ever in conflict. It is the age-long conflict between Satan and Christ with the Christian's life as the battleground. The two natures co-inhabit every believer throughout life (Galatians 5:16-17).

Our part in the conquest is clear-cut. We must condemn the flesh and have no confidence in it. We must consent to the crucifixion of "the old man". God has already crucified our old nature with Christ on the cross, but we must give our heart consent to the transaction and consider it an accomplished fact. We are to reckon ourselves dead to sin (Romans 6:11). Sin shall not have dominion over you (Romans 6:14). We are not fighting to win a victory, but we are celebrating the victory that has already been won!

We must make no provision for the flesh. Instead, we are told to renew our minds daily in the Word of God. We must meditate and listen to His word, allowing it to speak back to us. We must experience communion, worship, and adoration of our Lord. Prayer is vital to keeping our spiritual nature in place over our flesh. By sharing our faith and ministering to others we keep under our flesh.

We must make a choice: self (ego) in control of our lives or Christ reigning within us by His Spirit. When we consider ourselves to be dead (sharing in His crucifixion), we open the door to being alive in Him (sharing in His resurrection). A choice for the spiritual over the fleshly opens the way for the Holy Spirit living the life of Jesus in and through us.

We must ask to be filled with the Spirit. This is to come under the absolute control of Christ. There is a three-fold manifestation:

1. **The realization of Christ's abiding presence.**
2. **The reproduction of Christ's holy life (Galatians 5:22-23).**
3. **The re-enactment of Christ's supernatural power (John 14:17).**

We must yield unconditionally to Him – spirit, soul, and body. This means to live in total dependence on Christ, appropriating His life, in every decision and circumstance that comes up in our lives. The victorious life is brought about wholly by Christ. It is not sustained by our continued efforts, but through our continued receiving of His life. Christ's power is made futile by our own efforts. Christ's life is received by faith and thanksgiving to God.

To walk in the Spirit places us on the front lines of attack by the enemy, Satan. We are instructed to put on the whole armor of God daily (Ephesians 6:10-18). We are also told to bring every thought under scrutiny and into captivity to the obedience of Christ (Philippians 4:8). Thoughts lead to actions and actions lead to habits.

We are to ever keep in mind our position and authority in Christ. We are seated in the heavens with access to the courts of heaven, according to Ephesians 1:20-23, and Satan is a defeated foe. We have power over the entire enemy (Luke 10:19-20) through the name of Christ (His name represents all that He is) and by the blood of Christ (Revelation 12:10). We are not to strive to win the victory because it has already been won. Rather, we are to maintain the victory by faith. We stand on the Word of God.

In light of these truths we rejoice, for God has made ample provision for us, so that in our walk with Him through our daily lives, we are empowered by the Holy Spirit within us! Alone we cannot walk the Christian life, but He can. We cannot overcome sin or face crises or temptations alone, but our covenant companion, the Holy Spirit, can. He will do the walking for those of us who know our responsibility is to be in total dependence – a daily reliance upon – the ability and power of the Holy Spirit. He will perform His purpose within us, making real all that Christ is, all that He has done for us, and all that is ours in Him.

Conclusion on the Holy Spirit

Within the body of Christ we are to prepare, equip, and train the saints. This is an impossible task without the Holy Spirit. He is an essential element of the five-fold ministry in preparing the sheep (His people) for service.

To prepare is to arrange for, create, get ready to, make ready, provide, take precautions, train; readiness, foresight. How are we to prepare the body for ministry and service? Prayer and intimate time with God is the path for letting Him transform us into a vessel of honor and a witness by His love, grace, goodness and mercy to do His will.

The word equips means to furnish, outfit, and prepare one's mind with the Word of God and to get the passion for souls deep into your heart. God's word in us gives us authority to comprehend the times and seasons. Used as a sword to separate falsehoods from the truth is the power to transform the belief system into Christ-likeness – Jesus knew the Father and did only the Father's will. To train has to do with attendance, like a military procession. It is to study, to teach a beginner or recruit or student.

We must declare and decree the truth and the promises of God that apply to each situation. Shout to the Lord over yourself and home. Decree that you believe and serve the resurrected Christ. Allow yourself to be released as a polished arrow to take back what the enemy has stolen.

We must not forsake the studying of God's Word. We must ask God to lead us in how He would have our personal study be done. The study of His word is the plumb line of the heart of God to seek for treasures of silver and gold.

It is also very important and powerfully helpful to train ourselves to share our testimony with conviction and confidence. It is good for others to hear what God has done for each of us and how He did it. Great encouragement and hope can come to those who listen to what we tell about God's dealings with our own lives. Jesus said in John 14 that He gave us the Holy Spirit to remind us of all He has taught us. The disciples trusted this statement from Christ; we should, too.

Become a "sent one" by focusing on the goal to be used by God and to minister to God and to His people as He leads. Our faces must be set like flint to always be in line with His ways. We must believe that we are qualified in Christ, not letting anyone or any system or situation put on us the yoke of disqualification to share Christ. Yes, it is important for us to be submitted to authority and released when we are ready, but we must not believe lies when it comes to who qualified us – Jesus is our qualifier.

It is vital for us to know what our gifting's are and focus on maturing in them by being like Mary who sat at His feet, soaking up the treasures of His Word. One of the most powerful experiences I have had is letting God be God and letting go by trusting Him. Choosing to be faithful in the little things, we are promoted by God without having to strive for it.

There is a cost to obeying the unction of His voice. When He tells us to let go of a secular activity for a season – like playing bridge, tennis, coffee groups, obligations that pull us away from Him – it is amazing what He will do to meet us as we draw near to Him.

Conclusion

Men and women who have chosen to walk out the challenge and charge to be transformed by God's loving grace deserve the blessings and honor of His Covenant. Just as Ruth, David, Jonah, Mary, Solomon and many more faced their heart wounds, their traumas and mental anguish to see freedom and courage bring glory to God's divine plan and exchange, so can you dear reader.

Many will not understand the complexity of all types of abuse and how it leaves you devastated and fearful. I love the words in the new song sung by Lady Ga Ga at the 2016 Oscars "till it happens to you, you don't know how I feel."

The River of His love flowing from the pages of the bible to your heart and the power of the Kingdom gospel breaking through the walls of pride will bring a whole new world to your life.

The Holy Spirit desires to lead, guide and direct you in all truth to come to know the best friend and the most profound healer to your soul. He will make you into a beautiful priceless tapestry woven by the Master's hand to bring Him glory.

Meet the only one who can make a divine exchange – Jesus Christ, One and Only True God.

Love is the path to follow to learn how to flow in the Spirit.

ABOUT THE AUTHOR

Karen L. Johnson is an ordained minister since 1995 and shares the Kingdom gospel with power and authority. She has been to several nations and continues praying for open doors for such a time as this.

Karen founded the Victorious Life Foundation in 1992 and the Victorious Life Center in Elk City, 2009 which included a healing room and bible school. She is a survivor of abuse who turned to God for healing of the multiple traumas to include five near death experiences by choosing to look on the inside of her heart allowing truth to prevail. Karen ministers in personal prophecy and prophecies to leaders and nations for breakthrough. She desires to see the church walk in freedom of the healing power of God's love.

She especially enjoys praying for justice to be restored where injustice has prevailed using her authority in the courts of heaven. God has made her a warrior shining brightly back to Him.

Karen is married to Tom Johnson of Elk City, OK and they have 4 adult children, 6 grandchildren and 1 great-granddaughter.

Much credit is given to the host of powerful, obedient ministers for speaking into my life at the appointed time for me to continue to press on to the high calling in Christ Jesus.

Other books she has authored include and available on http://www.Amazon.com are:

1. **39 Gems, Walking with the Master**
2. **Valuable Oils of the Bible and their Prayerful Use**
3. **The Big Weight Loss Mind Game: Truth and Lies**
4. **Establish God's Kingdom in Your Field-Prayer**

Zephaniah 3:17 (AMPLIFIED):

"The LORD your God is in your midst."

A WARRIOR WHO SAVES.

He will rejoice over you with joy; He will be quiet in His love (making no mention of your past sins). He will rejoice over you with shouts of joy.

www.ingramcontent.com/pod-product-compliance
Lightning Source LLC
Chambersburg PA
CBHW071533040426
42452CB00008B/997